FRENCH PEORIA AND THE ILLINOIS COUNTRY
1673 – 1846

by
Judith A. Franke
Dickson Mounds Museum

Graphic Design
by
Eric Johnson

In cooperation with the
Peoria 1691 Foundation

With the support of
The City of Peoria
Mary Ann and Barry MacLean
David Ransburg

Illinois State Museum
Popular Science Series, Vol. XII

Illinois State Museum Society
Springfield, Illinois
1995

Library of Congress Cataloging–in–Publication Data

Franke, Judith A. 1937 –
    French Peoria and the Illinois Country, 1673 – 1846 / by Judith A. Franke; graphic
design by Eric Johnson; in cooperation with the Peoria 1691 Foundation.
        p. cm. – (Illinois State Museum popular science series, ISSN 0360–0297; vol. 12)
    Includes bibliographical references (p.) and index.
    ISBN 0–89792–140–2 (pbk)
    1. French–Illinois–Peoria–History. 2. French–Illinois–History. 3. Peoria (Ill.)–
History. 4. Illinois–History–To 1778. 5. Illinois–History–1778–1865. I. Peoria 1691
Foundation. II. Title. III. Series; Illinois State Museum popular science series; v. 12.
F549.P4F73 1995
977.3–dc20   95–19580
                                                                                                CIP

Contents

APPENDICES

Introduction

Many histories of Illinois begin at statehood, a little more than 150 years ago, when Americans — mostly of British descent — settled the area. These histories often ignore or only briefly touch upon the 150 years before that time, when the Illinois Country was explored and settled by the French. In commemoration of the three-hundredth year of European settlement at Peoria, this book is concerned with the little-known first half of its history.

Peoria was first the southernmost part of New France, then the northernmost part of the French Colony of Louisiana, and finally the westernmost part of the newly formed United States. It is interesting, therefore, that in the perception of many Americans today, Peoria is the quintessential middle American town.

French interests were dominant at Peoria for well over a hundred years, from the time the first French explorers came up the Illinois River in 1673 until the first "American" settlers began to move into the area in about 1815. A small French presence persisted for a time on the east bank of the river but was gone by about 1846. Today only faint echoes of French Peoria survive in the street plan of downtown Peoria, and in the name of an occasional street, school, or hotel meeting room — "Joliet," "Marquette," "LaSalle."

The French were not only gone from Peoria by the mid-19th century, they were forgotten by most Peorians and historians. Over the years, however, there were a few who persisted in the search for Peoria's French past. Several people became involved in the subject through their work on historical articles for the *Peoria Journal Star* or through involvement with the Peoria Historical Society. The most prominent of these was Ernest E. East, who was long associated with both organizations. For many years East collected information on French Peoria from widely scattered sources. He published a number of important journal and newspaper articles but never a complete synthesis of his findings. His valuable pamphlet listing the known inhabitants of French Peoria published in 1933 is reprinted here with the generous permission of his family (Appendix VII).

A brief glance at the pages that follow will show that this book was not written chiefly with scholars in mind — there are no footnotes. It is, on the other hand, the surprising end-product of a proposal that I made to the

Dickson Mounds Museum staff in 1989 to produce an exhibit on the French and the historic Indians of Illinois in conjunction with the Peoria Tricentennial celebration which was to begin in 1991. We felt that an exhibit on this theme would not only be timely but useful to the museum since we knew very little about the subject. Developing the exhibit would provide us with material to present to the public on a topic we had previously neglected in our interpretive programs.

Initially, most members of the museum staff were involved in project-related research — Alan Harn, Sharron Santure, Andrea Keller, Kelvin Sampson, and Duane Esarey as well as myself. Eventually Keller became more involved in locating and keeping track of the many books we borrowed, and Sampson became involved with production of the exhibit. Esarey and I remained the major researchers as the project progressed. We developed a special interest in the subject which continues to the present day, even though we are archaeologists, with a minimal knowledge of French.

We thought that a few months of research would provide the information needed. We found this material scattered in hundred-year-old histories, manuscript drafts and notes, and an array of newspaper clippings going back sixty years. The picture that this information yielded was full of major contradictions and gaps. Since we had more questions than answers, we next searched publications of original records — journals, memoirs, letters, and official reports — that recorded the historical events in question. Here we encountered even more mysteries, contradictions, obvious fabrications, and some incomprehensible "facts." By trial and error, and the advice of some experts in the field, we began to piece together a coherent story, which took form in the exhibit, "The Illinois Country, 1673 – 1846." The exhibit opened at the Dickson Mounds Museum in June of 1990 and traveled throughout Peoria during its Tricentennial year (from September 1991 to September 1992). By the end of the Tricentennial year we had been persuaded to rework the exhibit into book form.

Choosing Peoria as our focus led us early to the difficulty presented by a lack of original records. The Peoria settlement was not as large or structured as the Illinois Country towns of Kaskaskia, Cahokia, or Ste. Genevieve, and was often not even officially sanctioned as a post. If substantive legal or church records of French Peoria ever existed, they have disappeared over time. Some records relating to Peoria inhabitants do, however, occur among the records of contemporary settlements and in the French Colonial Archives.

It is difficult to document the lives of the inhabitants of early Peoria since the French of that time used aliases, abbreviated names, nicknames, or — since many were illiterate — spelled names in a variety of ways. Our choice of spellings in this book is sometimes arbitrary. When dealing with literate individuals, we have tried to spell their names as they themselves spelled them — thus "Jolliet," not "Joliet"; "Delliette," not "DeLiette" or "Desliette"; and "Tonti," not "Tonty" (if indeed it is an "i" in his signature, as some say, and not a "y" as it appears to be).

Place names at Peoria present their own difficulties. Fort Crèvecoeur was in existence for only a few months in 1680, but the name persisted on European-made maps for decades. Fort St. Louis, established at Peoria by Tonti in 1691, was never, to my knowledge, called by that name in documents or on maps. If noted at all, it was called "Fort Pimetoui," the "Fort of the French and Illinois Indians," or the "Old Fort." The Illinois Indians called the lake "Pimetoui," and this name was frequently used by the French for the lake or the post. The lake and the post were also called "Peoria," after the Illinois tribe most closely associated with the area. The narrows, several miles above the lower end of the lake, were called "Petit Détroit."

The French Peoria settlement itself was called by a variety of names which some scholars suggest refer to the town's location at the lower end or foot ("pied") of Lake Peoria. Some of the names that occur are "Au Pay," "Dupee," "Le Pe," "Opa," "Pays," "Pe," and "Pees." It seems clear that all of these names are corruptions of "Au Pe," a shortened French form of either "Peoria" or "Pimeteoui." Abbreviated names were commonly used by the French for their settlements. Post Vincennes was called "Au Post"; Kaskaskia, "Au Kas"; Cahokia, "Au Cahok"; and the Arkansas post, "Aux Arks" (Ozarks). We refer to some locations by their modern or anglicized names. The rock formation known to the French as "Le Rocher" is today called "Starved Rock" after an Indian tale, and we usually refer to it by that name.

The time period covered by this book was one of turmoil for the Indian tribes of the Illinois Country. We do not attempt to summarize the complex histories of these many tribes, but we have tried to generally follow the movements of the Peoria, the tribe most closely associated with the site of the city of Peoria, which still bears the tribe's name.

The lives of the historic tribes of the midwest revolved around planting, harvesting, hunting, and social activities organized according to a well-documented seasonal pattern. In early spring the tribe assembled in a summer agricultural village, planted crops, and then went on a communal buffalo hunt, returning to the village to harvest and store food. In the fall the group dispersed to several smaller winter villages from which it pursued more specialized hunting for several months. The final months of the winter were devoted to even smaller hunting campaigns as well as to gaming, dancing, and singing. In the spring the group assembled once again in its large summer village.

It is difficult to study the movements of the historic Indian tribes of the Illinois Country because one often cannot identify the geographic location of places referred to in documents, letters, and accounts. An account may state that an individual was sent to the Peoria or visited the Peoria at their village, but may not indicate where that village was located at the time. This is a critical problem in interpreting historic events in the Illinois Country since the French often resided with the Indians and moved with them.

Intensive documentary research by Duane Esarey since completion of the exhibit has enabled us to trace in considerable detail the seasonal residency patterns of post-contact tribes along the Illinois River. His study has been of great assistance in interpreting historical accounts.

When they descended the Mississippi River in 1673, Jolliet and Marquette found the Peoria in northeastern Missouri. Later that year they may have encountered them somewhere along the Illinois. After 1673 the Peoria apparently had their summer village at Le Rocher (Starved Rock), dispersing to winter villages at Lake Pimetoui and sites farther downstream on the Illinois River. In 1691 the French moved their post to Peoria in conjunction with the establishment of the Peoria summer village at that site. By about 1711 the Peoria had reestablished a summer village at Le Rocher while sometimes maintaining a second village at Peoria. Sometime between 1723 and the 1730s the tribe abandoned the Peoria area because of the Fox Wars, and moved their summer village to the area of Cahokia. They moved the village back to Peoria in the 1730s but had apparently left the Peoria area permanently by about 1750. During this entire period, they utilized a number of smaller village sites at other locations in the winter. A principal recurring winter village site of the Peoria and other Illinois tribes in the lower Illinois valley was located near modern Naples and Mauvaise Terre Creek.

Saint-Ange, the commandant at Fort de Chartres, wrote to the Commandant at Louisiana in August of 1764 that a Potawatomi chief forced the Peoria — then encamped on the Mississippi — to return horses and slaves which they had stolen from the French inhabitants "aux Peorias." By this date the Peoria tribe had left the site, but the French village retained the tribe's name.

The Naples site was occasionally referred to as "Mauvaise Terre." Peoria post commander Maillet wrote an official letter from there in January of 1781. Internal evidence indicates that he was at that time in the lower Illinois River valley, apparently wintering near the Potawatomi and Kickapoo.

In an 1898 interview in the *Peoria Journal* with early Peoria resident Adeline Chandler, she clearly refers to Peoria as "Mauvaise Terre." This ninety-year-old woman appears to be confused about events that occurred when she was six. The fact, however, that she did know this place name and associated it with Peoria probably indicates that she had at some point resided at the Mauvaise Terre site with her trader father. (She may have been born there in December of 1806.)

It is in the light of ongoing historical research that our "Chronology of Events at French Peoria" (Appendix VI) should be viewed. It is a working chronology, incorporating those facts that we know with some degree of certainty and upon which we have constructed our story.

This book, like the exhibit, includes reproductions of the signatures of a number of the principal subjects as well as portions of original documents, to remind readers of the source material upon which history is based. We also chose to feature certain individuals selected because of the significance of their accomplishments, or because their lives graphically reflect their times. Some of these people are well known — La Salle, Tonti, Jolliet, Marquette, and DuSable. Others are little known and of lesser note — Marie Rouensa, Maillet, Adeline Chandler, Chatellereau, and Buisson. One of them, Pierre Delliette, was of critical importance to the Illinois Country for 35 years but has been almost unknown to historians.

Many people helped us in many ways. These include John Walthall of the Illinois Department of Transportation; Eric Mack of Elsah, Illinois; John Aubrey, Jay Miller, and Helen Tanner of the Newberry Library, Chicago, Illinois; Molly McKenzie of Cahokia Courthouse, Cahokia, Illinois; Anton Pregaldin of Clayton, Missouri; Holly LiBaire of St. Clair County Historical Society, Belleville, Illinois; Nancy McCloud of Springfield, Illinois; Winston DeVille of Villa Platte, Louisiana; and Patricia Galloway of the Mississippi Department of Archives and History, Jackson, Mississippi.

Certain individuals deserve our special thanks. Richard Day of the Byron R. Lewis Historical Library of Vincennes disclosed and made available to us the mortgage document and 1796 probate of the estate of Louis Chatellereau — documents previously unknown to Peoria historians. Carl Ekberg, of Illinois State University — in addition to providing much helpful information — provided a great service by criticizing our thinking until it improved.

Since we are situated many miles from any library of note and do not have schedules which permit our frequenting distant libraries, we depended for most of our research on the Western Illinois Library System which delivered a stream of sometimes obscure publications directly to our door through their Interlibrary Loan Service. We also acknowledge the generous assistance of Lawrence Conrad of Western Illinois University, who lent us anything we wanted from his extraordinary personal library (including the "Jesuit Relations").

Individuals who contributed very directly to this publication include: Linda Hampton, Director of the Peoria 1691 Foundation who provided encouragement and support; Rex Linder of the Foundation who assisted with some details of publication and funding; Logan Printing of Peoria which made a significant subvention in printing costs; Orvetta Robinson, Edward A. Munyer, and Bonnie Styles, of the Illinois State Museum; and Lois Menzel of Northfield, Minnesota, who provided very significant editorial assistance. Major assistance with the publication was given by Betty Fawcett, Kim White, and Jeannette Vaultonburg of the Dickson Mounds Museum staff; Amy Mitchell of the Illinois State Museum; and particularly by volunteer Bill Cook of St. David, Illinois. The City of Peoria, Mary Ann and Barry MacLean of Libertyville, and David Ransburg of Peoria provided much-needed financial assistance. The contribution by Eric Johnson of his professional skills in the graphic design of the book represents an extraordinary volunteer effort. Finally, special thanks must go to Duane Esarey who served as discussant and sounding board and answered my daily questions throughout the project.

From exhibit to book, this project would never have developed as it did without the interest and assistance of Peoria's Gloria LaHood. The constant behind-the-scenes activity of this dedicated woman with (to quote her), "no credentials!" was crucial to the resurrection of French Peoria from the dark ages in which it had languished, through the revitalization of the Tricentennial, to the lively subject it has become today. My first vivid memory of the project is sitting with Gloria on the floor of her study in 1989 surrounded by hundreds of pieces of paper — all the obscure bits of Peoria history which had come her way over the years and which she had squirreled away. A culminating memory is meeting the Chief of the Peoria tribe and other tribal representatives in 1992 when they officially visited Peoria after a 240-year absence as guests of the Peoria Tricentennial Pow Wow, "Return to Pimiteoui."

Judith A. Franke
Dickson Mounds Museum

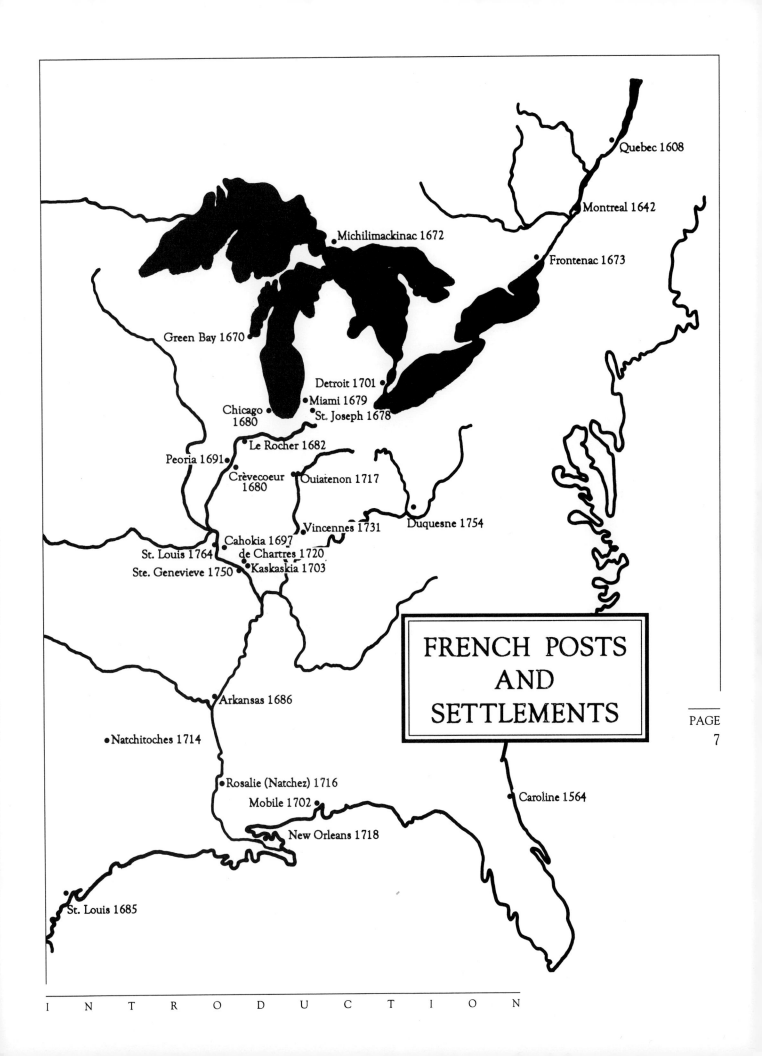

Quebec 1608

Montreal 1642

Michilimackinac 1672

Frontenac 1673

Green Bay 1670

Detroit 1701
Miami 1679
Chicago
1680
St. Joseph 1678

Le Rocher 1682

Peoria 1691

Crèvecoeur
1680
Ouiatenon 1717

Vincennes 1731
Duquesne 1754

Cahokia 1697
St. Louis 1764
de Chartres 1720
Ste. Genevieve 1750
Kaskaskia 1703

Arkansas 1686

Natchitoches 1714

FRENCH POSTS
AND
SETTLEMENTS

Rosalie (Natchez) 1716
Mobile 1702
Caroline 1564
New Orleans 1718

St. Louis 1685

First Encounters

The French in the Illinois Country in the Late 1600s.

France began its explorations of North America in the 1500s and in the 1600s established the province of New France along the St. Lawrence River in Canada. After exploring the Mississippi River and its tributaries in the late 1600s, in 1699 the French established the province of Louisiana on the lower Mississippi. The area where the two provinces met was called "The Illinois Country" after the Illinois tribes that lived there. As the southern part of New France and then the northern part of Louisiana, the Illinois Country was a hinterland of these French colonies for a century prior to becoming part of the American frontier.

The Illinois Country was involved in a series of political upheavals — the French and Indian War, the American Revolution, the War of 1812, and then the settling of the West. By the early 1800s, the conflicts between French, British, Spanish, Americans, and Indians had resulted in the area being lost by the French and the Indians and controlled by the United States. However, the French heritage of Illinois continued to be strong well into the 1800s.

The American Indians who lived in Illinois during the French colonial period were members of many different tribes, some closely related by language and custom, and others not. All were unsettled by the pressure of European settlement — the Spanish came from the south and southwest, the British from the east and southeast, the French from the northeast — each nation recruiting certain tribes as trading partners or allies against other nations.

The French were few in number and different in character. They came to the New World for power, wealth, land, freedom, and adventure, or to convert the American Indians to Christianity. Some were aristocrats or of the lesser nobility, well educated and sophisticated. Others were middle class artisans, soldiers, and craftsmen. Still others were illiterate peasant farmers or laborers.

•

LOUIS JOLLIET AND
JACQUES MARQUETTE

L. Jolliet   *Jacque marquette*

Born:	1645, Québec.	1637, Laon, France.
Parents:	French Canadian. Father a wheelwright.	From an ancient and illustrious family.
Education:	Attended College of Jesuits, Québec, for 11 years.	Attended College of Jesuits in France for 20 years. Ordained 1666.
Special Talents:	Cathedral organist.	Indian languages.
Experience Previous to Voyage:	Visited France. Fur trader.	Teacher. Missionary to Great Lakes Indians for six years.
Experience After Voyage:	Fur trader. Explored Hudson Bay and Labrador area. Married Claire Byssot.	Returned briefly to found mission among the Illinois at Starved Rock.
Died:	1700, New France.	1675, Western Michigan.

•

*He possesses tact
and prudence,
[and] has the
courage to dread
nothing where
everything is
to be feared.
(Jolliet
described by
Father Dablon)*

•

•

*This painting on
wood, apparently dating
to 1669 and inscribed with
Marquette's name, was
discovered in Montréal in 1897 and
may be an authentic portrait.*

Although the De Soto Expedition reached the southern end of the Mississippi River in 1541, the river was still unexplored a hundred years later when French missionaries on the Great Lakes were told by Indians of a great mid-continental river. In 1673 the Governor of New France authorized a young fur trader, Louis Jolliet, to explore this river, which he hoped would lead to the Pacific. Jolliet was accompanied on this journey by the Jesuit missionary Jacques Marquette and five others.

The party of explorers entered the upper Mississippi River from the Wisconsin River (Pl. I). In what is now Missouri, they found several villages of Illinois Indians. They stayed for several days with the Peoria tribe at a village that had over three hundred houses.

When Jolliet and Marquette reached the confluence of the Missouri and Mississippi Rivers, they saw two monsters painted on a high bluff along the river.

They have horns on their heads like those of a deer, a horrible look, red eyes, a beard like a tiger's, a face somewhat like a man's, a body covered with scales, and so long a tail that it winds all around the body, passing above the head and going back between the legs, ending in a fish's tail.... Green, red and black are the three colors. (Marquette's Journal)

Piasa from a 1678 Franquelin Map.

Five years after the voyage, the mapmaker Franquelin drew the creature at the upper right — called a "piasa" by the Indians — on a map that he made in Canada. Although no drawings by Jolliet or Marquette survive, La Salle speaks of having seen a drawing of the piasa by Jolliet, and it is possible that the mapmaker saw this drawing as well.

From a Marquette letter, 1666.

After descending the Mississippi River to the Arkansas, the explorers realized that the course of the river would be to the Gulf of Mexico. They returned up the Mississippi and Illinois Rivers, where they encountered the Kaskaskia tribe of the Illinois at Starved Rock (Pl. II).

In a note at the end of his journal, Marquette says that he baptized a dying child at the village of the Peoria tribe where they spent three days on their return trip. He does not say where they encountered this tribe, but it was apparently not at Starved Rock. Since the only other place the Peoria are known to have stayed in the area at about this time was at Peoria Lake, Marquette and Jolliet may have been the first to encounter them there.

His gentleness ... made him beloved by all, and made him all things to all men — a Frenchman with the French, a Huron with the Hurons, an Algonquin with the Algonquins ... the childlike candor with which he disclosed his heart to his superiors and even to all kinds of persons, with an ingenuousness which won all hearts. (Marquette described by his superior, Father Dablon)

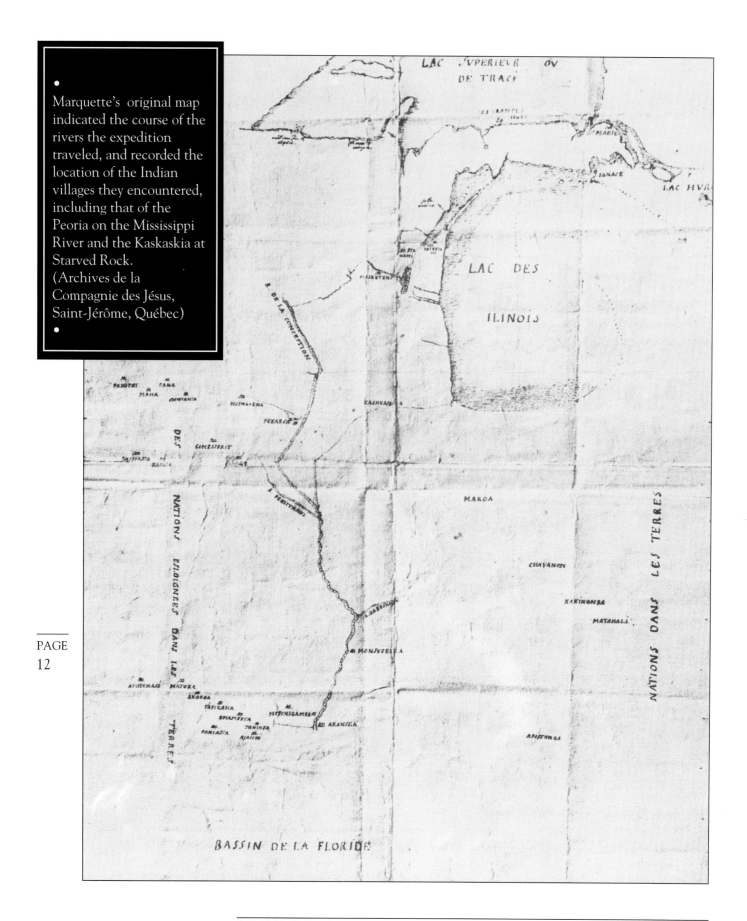

• Marquette's original map indicated the course of the rivers the expedition traveled, and recorded the location of the Indian villages they encountered, including that of the Peoria on the Mississippi River and the Kaskaskia at Starved Rock. (Archives de la Compagnie des Jésus, Saint-Jérôme, Québec) •

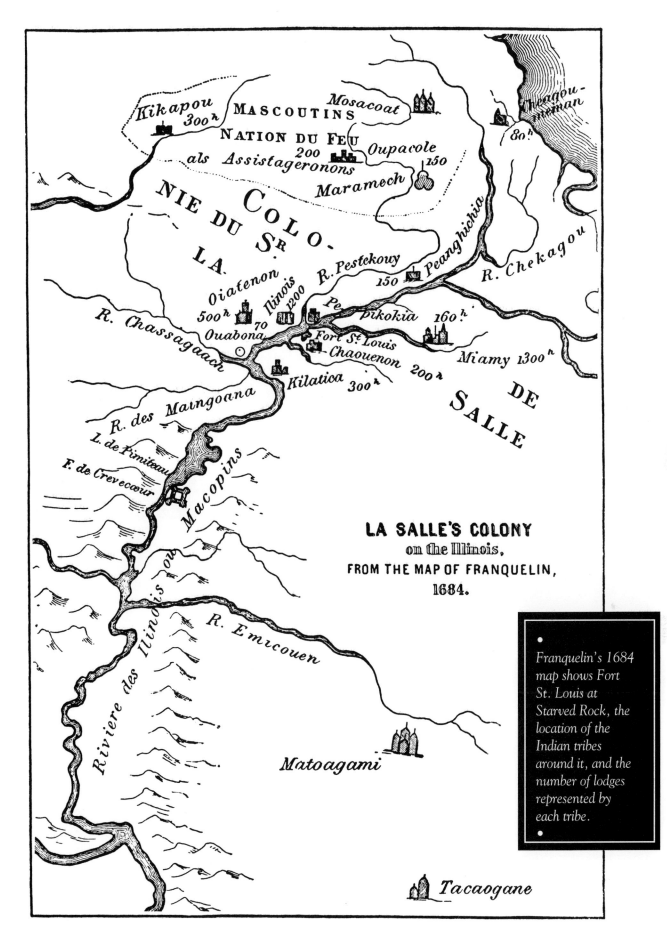

Kikapou
300ᴸ

MASCOUTINS

Mosacoat

Meagoutiteman
80ᴸ

NATION DU FEU
als Assistageronons
200
Oupacole
150

Maramech

COLO-
NIE DU Sʀ.
LA.

R. Chassagaach

Oiatenon
500ᴸ
70
Ouabona

Illinois
1200

R. Pestekouy

Peanghichia
150

R. Chekagou

Pe   Pikokia   160ᴸ

Fort Sᵗ Louis
Chaouenon 200ᴸ

Miamy 1300ᴸ

DE
SALLE

Kilatica 300ᴸ

R. des Maingoana

L. de Pimiteau

F. de Crevecœur

Macopins

LA SALLE'S COLONY
on the Illinois,
FROM THE MAP OF FRANQUELIN,
1684.

R. Emicouen

Riviere des Ilinois ou

Matoagami

Tacaogane

Franquelin's 1684
map shows Fort
St. Louis at
Starved Rock, the
location of the
Indian tribes
around it, and the
number of lodges
represented by
each tribe.

ROBERT CAVELIER, SIEUR DE LA SALLE

Born:	1643, Rouen, France.
Parents:	Influential merchant family.
Education:	Private tutors. Attended Jesuit college in France for seven years.
Special Interests:	Geography, history, religion, mathematics.
Experience:	Teacher, manager of farm estate in New France, fur trader, commandant of Fort Frontenac, explorer.
Major Achievements:	Exploration of the Mississippi River to its mouth (claiming mid-continent for France). Granted title of nobility and rights to land he explored by Louis XIV.
Later Experience:	Unsuccessfully led expedition from France to Gulf of Mexico to found colony at mouth of Mississippi.
Died:	1687. Killed by his men at Trinity River, Texas.

Conjectural Portrait, G.P.A. Healy; Chicago Historical Society.

Some individuals have a renown that seems out of proportion to their actual accomplishments. Such a man was Robert Cavelier, Sieur de La Salle whose deeds and personality made a lasting impression on those who knew him. Some thought him a genius and others a fool.

After study with private tutors in France, La Salle began training as a Jesuit, hoping for a life of adventure in foreign missions. However, he was considered too individualistic and independent to represent the order abroad. At 22 he left the Jesuit order and sailed for North America.

The next twelve years of La Salle's life in New France are difficult to follow in detail. He spent several years developing a small estate at Québec. He associated with fur traders, missionaries, and Indians who told about unexplored lands to the west and south; and he travelled in the wilderness for long periods in the company of these men. He eventually helped the Governor of New France develop an audacious plan to claim the entire mid-continent for France through exploration of the great south-flowing river — to open up a southern route for trade and to establish posts and settlements along this route. To achieve this end, he obtained extraordinary favors from Louis XIV — a nobleman's title, command of Fort Frontenac on Lake Ontario, permission to explore the lands to the south, and rights to the lands he discovered.

La Salle brought 30 craftsmen, seamen, and assistants from France for his expedition, including Henri de Tonti, a young officer from a prominent Italian family. At Niagara in mid-winter they built the *Griffon*, the first ship to sail the Great Lakes (Pl. III). They sailed to the mouth of Green Bay and sent some of the men with the ship back to Niagara with furs. It was never seen again. In 1679 the expedition traveled up the St. Joseph River and down the Kankakee and Illinois, arriving in January at Lake Peoria (Pl. IV) where it encountered a large encampment of Illinois Indians (Pl. V). After hearing alarming tales from these Indians, six men deserted.

A few miles downstream from the Peoria village, La Salle's party built a small fort called Crèvecoeur and began construction of a 42-foot boat in which to descend the river. The drawing below is based on La Salle's detailed description of the fort's construction.

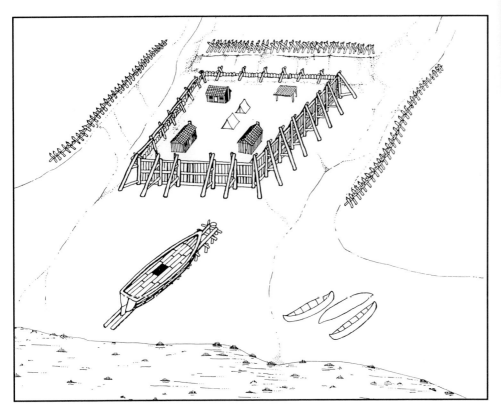

The fear of making mistakes makes me more reserved than I like to be, so I rarely expose myself to conversation with those in whose company I am afraid of making blunders, and can hardly help making them …. If I am wanting in expansiveness and show of feeling towards those with whom I associate, it is only through a timidity which is natural to me, and which made me leave various employments, where without it, I should have succeeded. (La Salle described by himself)

Reconstruction drawing of Fort Crèvecoeur. Dickson Mounds Museum.

Later in the winter La Salle sent Father Hennepin, Michel Accault, and a third man to explore the upper reaches of the Mississippi River. He sent Tonti with several men to explore the site of Starved Rock. He took five men overland 1,300 miles to Fort Frontenac for additional supplies (Pl. VI). The small group of men left at Crèvecoeur deserted the fort. Tonti and the Illinois tribes at Starved Rock were attacked by the Iroquois (Pl. VII).

In January 1682 the expedition, consisting of 23 Frenchmen and 18 Indians, set out once again from Lake Michigan to explore the Mississippi River (Pl. VIII). In early February they entered the Mississippi River from the Illinois (Pl. IX). In March they passed the farthest point reached by Jolliet and Marquette. On April 9, 1682 La Salle erected a cross at the mouth of the Mississippi River and claimed it for France (Pl. X).

> *In the name of the most high, mighty, invincible, and victorious Prince, Louis the Great . . . Fourteenth of that name, I, this ninth day of April, one thousand six hundred and eighty-two, in virtue of the commission of his Majesty, which I hold in my hand . . . take possession of this country of Louisiana . . . from the mouth of the great river called the Ohio, as far as its mouth at the sea.*

On returning upriver, La Salle and his men built Fort St. Louis at Starved Rock.

Two years later, La Salle, with four ships, sailed from France to the Gulf of Mexico in an attempt to establish a colony at the mouth of the Mississippi River. After several years of accumulated disasters, he was killed by his men. One of the few survivors of this expedition made this drawing of one of the expedition's ships, the *Joly*. (Archivo General de Indias, Seville)

> *He had a capacity and talent to make enterprise successful; his constancy and courage, and his extraordinary knowledge in arts and sciences, which rendered him fit for anything, together with an indefatigable body, which made him surmount all difficulties, would have procured a glorious issue to his undertaking, had not all those excellent qualities been counterbalanced by too haughty a behavior, which sometimes made him insupportable, and by a rigidness towards those that were under his command, which at last drew on him implacable hatred, and was the occasion of his death.* (Henri Joutel, La Salle's Lieutenant in the Gulf Expedition)

The French and Indians at Peoria — 1691 to 1763

The Legacy of La Salle

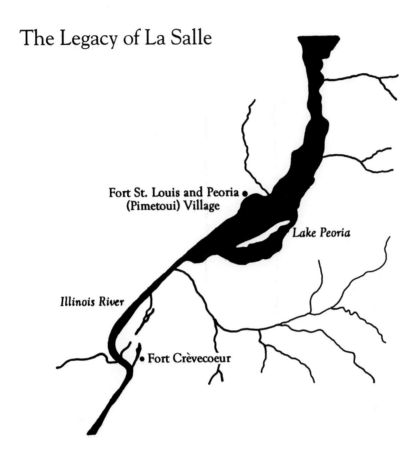

La Salle had opened the heart of North America to France, providing a link with its Caribbean holdings and driving a wedge between the English and Spanish possessions; but at the time of La Salle's death, this vast territory was unconsolidated. It was left to those who followed to create a thriving colony. For twenty-five years his successors worked to establish viable military and trading outposts and missions in the Illinois Country.

•
Location of early sites at Peoria associated with the French.

In 1690, Henri de Tonti, La Salle's lieutenant, inherited La Salle's trading and settlement rights along the Illinois which he supervised from Fort St. Louis, his post at Starved Rock. Helping him with this enterprise were his cousins, François Dauphin de La Forest and Pierre Delliette, and the explorer and trader, Michel Accault. Nearby were the villages of the Illinois tribes, including the Kaskaskia, with its chief, Rouensa, and his daughter Marie. Ministering to the tribes was the Jesuit missionary, Jacques Gravier. In 1691, all of these individuals moved downriver to establish a new settlement at Lake Pimetoui (Peoria). The events of their lives reflect the forces that were at work shaping the Illinois Country for a quarter century.

·

HENRI DE TONTI

·
*Tonti of the Iron Hand.
Nicholas Maes, Amsterdam, 1688;
Museum of the City of Mobile. The
painting incorrectly shows his left
hand missing.*

Born:	1649 or 1650, Italy or France.
Parents:	Eldest son of Lorenzo de Tonti and Isabelle di Lietto of Naples. Prominent Italian banking family living in France.
Education:	Unknown. Probably privately educated.
Experience:	Entered French Army at 18 and served for ten years in army and navy. Right hand blown off by grenade in Sicily. Taken prisoner and exchanged. Joined La Salle's expedition in Paris as his lieutenant.
Achievements:	Accompanied La Salle on expedition to mouth of Mississippi and became heir to his trading concessions. Maintained trading operations on the Illinois, Mississippi, and Great Lakes for 15 years. Negotiated and maintained relationships with Indian tribes, led troops in wars against Iroquois, established Fort St. Louis at Peoria and a post on the Arkansas. Commandant at Fort St. Louis, Old Mobile. Traveled through more of North America than perhaps any other explorer.
Died:	1704, at Old Mobile, of yellow fever.

Henri de Tonti is arguably one of the most important explorers of the Americas to have gone almost unnoticed by history. La Salle's "right hand man" had ironically lost his right hand in battle and wore a metal replacement. He got along well with La Salle, whom so many found difficult, and early in their collaboration, La Salle wrote of him to the Prince de Conti:

> *His honorable character and his amiable disposition were well-known to you, but perhaps you would not have thought him capable of doing things for which a strong constitution, an acquaintance with the country and the use of both hands seemed absolutely necessary. Nevertheless, his energy and address make him equal to anything.*

Because of his military background, La Salle gave Tonti primary responsibility for supervising the building of the *Griffon*, Fort Conti at Niagara, Fort Miami, the fort and boat at Crèvecoeur, and Fort St. Louis at Starved Rock.

In 1680, shortly after Tonti was sent by La Salle from Fort Crèvecoeur to Starved Rock to plan the building of a fort, Tonti heard of the desertion of Crèvecoeur and returned to salvage what he could. On his return to the Indian village at the Rock, Tonti and the Illinois were attacked by 600 Iroquois (Pl. VII). While trying to negotiate peace, Tonti was stabbed and nearly killed. He and his men escaped and, after an extremely difficult journey, reached Green Bay.

Tonti was second in command of La Salle's 1682 expedition to the mouth of the Mississippi. On their return they consolidated their position at Fort St. Louis on Starved Rock and encouraged tribes from a wide area to settle nearby. Tonti was left in command when La Salle went to France seeking support for an expedition by sea to the Gulf. Hearing in 1686 that La Salle had arrived in the Gulf, Tonti descended the Mississippi in an unsuccessful attempt to join him. Hearing in 1689 of La Salle's death, Tonti led a party as far as Texas in an unsuccessful search for survivors.

Tonti and his cousin La Forest were granted exclusive rights to Illinois trade after La Salle's death. In exchange for these rights, they were to maintain Fort St. Louis at Starved Rock, "with the charge to set the Illinois and neighboring nations against the Iroquois."

> *He is beloved by all the voyageurs. It was with deep regret that we parted from him. He is the man who best knows the country. He is loved and feared everywhere. (Description of Tonti by the priest St. Cosme.)*

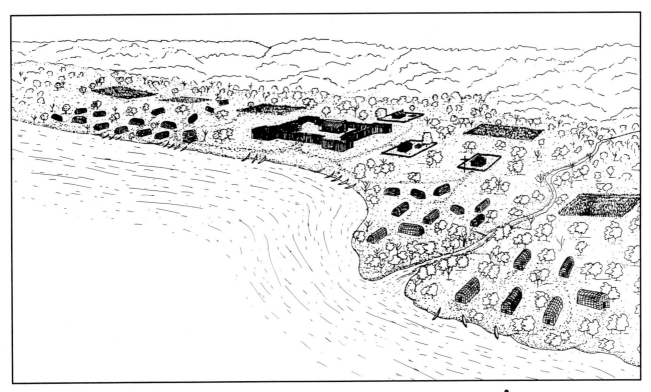

This reconstruction depicts the Indian village at Lake Peoria, Fort St. Louis, and the Mission of the Immaculate Conception. Dickson Mounds Museum.

In 1691, they moved their fort downriver from Starved Rock to Lake Pimetoui. Here, at the site of modern Peoria, they built another Fort St. Louis, where they were joined by the Illinois tribes and the Jesuit Mission.

THE FRENCH AND INDIANS AT PEORIA — 1691 TO 1763

Tonti was the primary figure in the fur trade in the Illinois Country for 20 years, doing everything possible to develop an efficient and profitable trade. He traveled some 85,000 miles by canoe and on foot negotiating with Indian tribes, discovering new sources of supply, hiring and supervising voyageurs, and struggling with the regulations and restrictions of the French bureaucracy.

By 1684 Tonti had established a small company of voyageurs who made regular trips between Fort St. Louis and Canada. Tonti furnished canoes, trade goods, and ammunition. The cost of these was deducted from the value of furs taken to market and the remaining profit was divided equally.

On July 17, 1689, a notary in Montréal compiled a list of merchandise given to four French voyageurs employed by Tonti and La Forest. The goods were taken to the Illinois Country and traded to the Indians for beaver pelts which the voyageurs delivered to Montréal.

Commodities, listed along with their values in the document, are cloth, clothing, blankets, guns, powder, lead, balls, musket-flints, tools, hatchets and knives, brandy and tobacco, bacon and hard bread, peas, quills, arrow-heads, kettles, needles and thread, mirrors, soap, beads, and paint.

French Trapper. Frederick Remington, 1891; Buffalo Bill Historical Center; Cody, Wyoming.

Detail of 1689 trade document. Chicago Historical Society

Although the fur trade seemed sucessful, the costs of trade goods, insurance, and shipping were too high for the trade to be profitable. When the Illinois trade was limited by the King to two canoes a year in 1696, Tonti began to look southward to the colony of Louisiana for opportunities. In 1700 he wrote:

> *What to do? There is no more trade since it has been forbidden by the court. All the voyages I made for the success of this country have ruined me.*

Since Tonti had lost his right hand, he usually dictated letters and documents. The document transferring his remaining shares in trading operations at Peoria's Fort St. Louis to his brother is an exception. Tonti says in the 1698 manuscript, "I have made and signed [it] with my own hand."

Tonti left Peoria for the last time in 1702 and died of yellow fever while commandant at Old Mobile in 1704. His memoirs, which have survived intact, are a clear and simple statement of fact, unadorned with drama or picturesque descriptions of landscape, wildlife, or Indian lifeways.

•
Tonti Manuscript.
Facsimile; Louisiana State Museum Historical Center.

Cultures in Conflict — Peoria in 1694

There are two detailed memoirs of events at Pimetoui in 1694 — one by the missionary Gravier and another by Tonti's cousin Delliette. They provide a wealth of detail on the daily activities and cultural complexity of the early years of this remote outpost.

•

J A C Q U E S   G R A V I E R

Born:	1651, Moulins, France.
Education:	Attended Jesuit College and taught in France for 15 years. Ordained. Studied Algonquin language in New France.
Special Interests:	Theology and canonical studies.
Major Achievements:	Missionary to the Illinois for 15 years at Starved Rock and Peoria. Wrote a grammar and dictionary of the Illinois language and detailed accounts of his mission.
Died:	1708, Old Mobile, of complications from wounds received at the hand of a Peoria Indian in 1705.

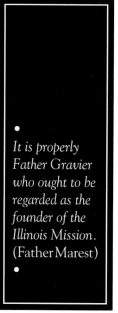

It is properly Father Gravier who ought to be regarded as the founder of the Illinois Mission. (Father Marest)

The missionary to succeed Jacques Marquette at Starved Rock was Jacques Gravier. In 1691 Gravier moved with the French and the Illinois to Peoria where he established the Mission of the Immaculate Conception.

> *I blessed the new chapel, which is built outside the fort, at a spot very convenient for the savages. On the eve before blessing the chapel and the cross, which is nearly 35 feet high, I invited the French to be good enough to be present. They promised to be there, and to manifest in public the honor in which they held it. They showed the savages by four volleys from their guns their veneration for this symbol of salvation.*

Father Gravier had his differences with the French traders:

> *There are among them some libertines who do not love the Missionary's presence, because they wish to continue their evil conduct.*

He also speaks in his letters about his difficulties with the Indians:

> *I was surprised by the indifference to instruction that I observed among the Peoria, notwithstanding the politeness with which the old men received me, one of them told me in confidence that his tribesmen had resolved to prevent the people from coming to the chapel to listen to me, because I spoke against their customs.*

> *Many children and young people were sick, and I had not as free access to all of them as I would have wished. Some are so prejudiced by the medicine men that, through fear that I may give them medicine, they say that they are quite well and disapprove of my frequent visits. They cry out against me as if I were the cause of the disease.... I was looked upon in most of the cabins as the bird of death; and people sought to hold me responsible for the disease and the mortality.*

•
Missionary.
Frederick Remington;
Buffalo Bill Historical Center;
Cody, Wyoming.

Gravier had his greatest success in the conversion of the young girls of the tribe. One of these, Marie, daughter of Chief Rouensa of the Kaskaskia, became the focus of controversy in the village.

> *She answered her father and mother, when they brought her to me in company with the Frenchman whom they wished to have for a son-in-law, [Michel Accault] that she did not wish to marry; that she had already given all her heart to God, and did not wish to share it.... I told [her parents and Michel Accault] that God did not command her not to marry, but also that she could not be forced to do so.... The father... told me that inasmuch as I was preventing his daughter from obeying him, he would also prevent her from going to the chapel. [He then threw Marie out of the lodge.]*

That very night her father gathered the chiefs of the four villages, and told them that, since I prevented the French from forming alliances with them… he earnestly begged them to stop the women and children from coming to the chapel. [Some girls, including Marie, did come to the chapel, but the chiefs disrupted the service.]

I thought I should not remain silent after so great an insult had been offered to God. I went to the commandant of the fort… [probably Delliette], *who answered in an insulting manner that I had drawn all this upon myself, through my stubbornness in not allowing the girl to marry the Frenchman, who was then with him.* [Gravier demanded that the commandant support him against the chiefs.] *He replied coldly that he would speak to the chiefs; but, instead of assembling them at once, he waited until the afternoon of the following day, and even then I had to return to him for the purpose.*

Marie held out against the many threats by her father. She was advised by Father Gravier:

My daughter, God does not forbid you to marry; neither do I say to you: 'Marry or do not marry.' If you consent solely through love for God, and if you believe that by marrying you will win your family to God, the thought is a good one.

The 17-year-old Marie Rouensa married Accault who spent almost 30 years of his adult life in the New World. He had been a member of La Salle's expedition, was captured by Indians in Wisconsin with Father Hennepin, and was a partner in the Peoria fur-trading enterprise. With the marriage, Accault is said to have reformed his "scandalous behavior."

Entry in the Kaskaskia Church records of baptism at Peoria in 1695 of the son of Michel Accault and Marie Rouensa. Diocese of Belleville, Illinois

Delliette, who was probably acting commandant in Tonti's absence at the time of this incident, speaks in his memoir of the cultural climate in which this incident took place:

> Although this nation is much given to debauchery, especially the men, the reverend Jesuit fathers, who speak their language perfectly, manage (if one may say so) to impose some check on this by instructing a number of girls in Christianity, who often profit by their teaching, and mock at the superstitions of their nation. This often greatly incenses the old men and daily exposes these fathers to ill-treatment, and even to being killed. I must say to their glory that they must be saints indeed to take as much trouble as they do for these people.

Gravier began to compile a dictionary and grammar of the language of the Illinois tribes when he arrived at Starved Rock in 1689. It is one of the few records of the language that survives.

A portion of Jacques Gravier's Dictionary of the Algonquin language of the Illinois. Watkinson Library, Trinity College, Hartford, CT.; and the Newberry Library.

Father Gravier worked among the Illinois at Peoria over a period of 14 years. In 1705 he was shot by a Peoria Indian and eventually died of his wounds.

•
MARIE ROUENSA

Born:	About 1678, at the Indian village at Starved Rock.
Parents:	Daughter of Chief Rouensa of the Kaskaskia tribe of the Illinois.
Education:	None, except from missionaries.
Major Events in Life: in	Converted to Christianity by Father Gravier at Peoria. In 1694, married Michel Accault, a French trader and explorer. Moved downriver to Indian village near Cahokia
	1700. Moved to French Kaskaskia and married trader Michel Philippe in 1703. Mother of eight children.
Died:	1725, French Kaskaskia.

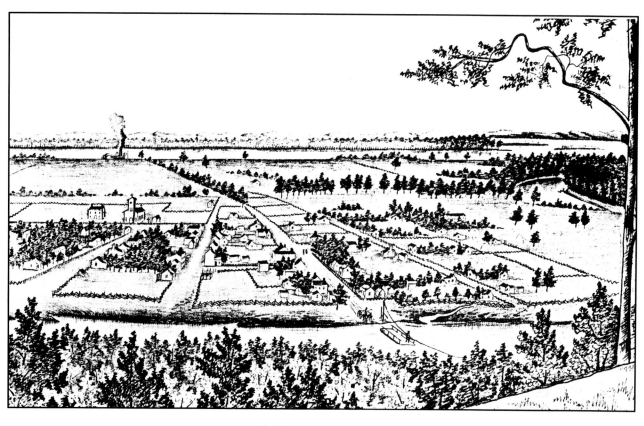

•
Pencil sketch of view of Kaskaskia. State Historical Society of Wisconsin.

The first of two sons born to Marie and Michel Accault was baptized in Peoria in 1695. In 1700 the family moved to an Indian village near Cahokia. By 1704, Marie had given birth to the first of six children born after her marriage to a second French trader, Michel Philippe, at the newly established town of French Kaskaskia, where Philippe became a farmer and Marie continued to be very active in the church.

In her will, dictated to her priest on her deathbed, Marie disposed
of her considerable estate, which included one Indian and five black slaves, to her
children. She disinherited her second son by Accault because he chose to live the
life of an Indian. A week later, she stipulated in a codicil that this son would
receive his share of her property if he reformed his ways. She asked that her will
be translated from French into the Illinois language. She was buried beneath her
pew in the Kaskaskia parish church.

Portion of codicil of will
of Marie Rouensa.
Courtesy Carl J. Ekberg.

•
PIERRE DELLIETTE

Born:	About 1665, France.
Parents:	Influential Italian expatriots. His father was probably the brother of Isabelle de Lietto, the wife of Lorenzo de Tonti.
Education:	Unknown, but probably privately educated.
Experience:	Linguist, Fur Trader, Officer, Commandant of forts and outposts. Negotiator between French and Indians.
Major Achievements:	Maintained frontier outposts, trading operations, and French and Indian relations in the Illinois Country at Starved Rock, Peoria, and Chicago for 35 years. Wrote detailed account of lifeways of the Illinois Indians.
Died:	Perhaps among the Natchez in Louisiana in 1721.

Delliette

An Italian raised in France among the nobility, Delliette joined his cousin Henri de Tonti at Fort St. Louis, Starved Rock, in 1687, and shortly afterward went on a five-week buffalo hunt with the Illinois. In 1705 he wrote the detailed account of his life among the Illinois tribes which is one of the most objective and nonjudgmental records of the lifeways of the Illinois Indians which exists. Delliette says in his memoir that his request to go on the hunt was readily granted by Tonti, because he was:

•
Buffalo Chase in Snowdrifts, Indians Pursuing on Snowshoes. George Catlin; 1832–33; Gilcrease Institute.

> *Pleased to have me learn this language, for which task he saw I had some talent, that he might safely absent himself when his affairs demanded it, and leave me in his place.... It was very easy for me, in view of my extreme youth, to learn the language of this nation.*

Delliette was to spend over 30 years — the rest of his life — living and working in the Illinois Country at posts at Starved Rock, Peoria, and Chicago. Between 1703 and 1711, he was the only French agent in the area. The eight years between 1712 and 1720 were a time of turmoil for Delliette and the Illinois Country. Incursions by the Fox threatened both the Illinois Indians and French trade. Delliette was employed by France as the chief negotiator between these warring parties.

In 1715 the Governor at Québec gave Delliette eight soldiers and a sergeant to reestablish a fort on the Illinois. This post may be that identified by archaeologists as the Newell Fort at Starved Rock. In 1719, however, Delliette was again at Peoria where he and Father de Kérében redeemed and returned Fox prisoners taken by the Peoria. In 1717 the Illinois Country became a part of the province of Louisiana. In 1718 Louisiana appointed Boisbriant Governor of the Illinois Country and the Fox War erupted in full force. The Illinois fled south.

The date and place of Pierre Delliette's death are not known. In June of 1721, Delliette was given permission in Québec to take two canoes to the "west." Those who traveled the Illinois later that year, however, did not encounter him. The historian Charlevoix says that he died before December of 1721 while negotiating a peace with the Natchez on behalf of the Governor of Louisiana. There is no evidence to confirm this statement. The earliest that anyone called Delliette is attested at the Natchez settlement is July of 1723. By the autumn of that year Charles Henri Joseph de Tonti, Henri de Tonti's nephew, is at the Natchez settlement and is calling himself "Desliettes."

•

I know of no officer better fitted for [establishing a post on the Illinois] *than Sieur Delliette, who understands and speaks the language of the Illinois with whom he has lived a long time.* (Governor of Québec, writing of Delliette)

•

•

Three Peouarea (Peoria) Indians. George Catlin, 1831. Iliniwek, Vol. 11, No. 2, 1973.

Delliette was the most ubiquitous French presence in the Illinois Country for more than 30 years. From the time that posts were established at Starved Rock in Peoria until the Illinois Country became a part of Louisiana, he oversaw the daily operations of the French posts and interactions with the tribes.

The People the French Encountered

The Indians the French encountered in the Illinois Country were principally those of the Illinois tribe, which included the Cahokia, Chepoussa, Chinkoa, Coiracoentanon, Espeminkia, Kaskaskia, Maroa, Michigamea, Moingwena, Peoria, Tamaroa, and Tapouaro. Tribes other than the Illinois encountered in the area were Fox, Kickapoo, Miami, Potawatomi, Sauk, Shawnee, Winnebago, Mascouten, and Iroquois.

Tonti's cousin Delliette came from France to the Illinois Country in 1687 as a very young man and spent the rest of his life with the Indians at Peoria, Starved Rock, Chicago, and other posts. Delliette quickly learned the languages and customs of the Illinois tribes and in 1705 wrote a memoir describing what he had learned about their lifeways in the years he spent living and working among them.

Detail of Delliette's Memoir, 1705; De Gannes copy; Newberry Library; E.E. Ayer Collection.

THE BUFFALO HUNT

The next day we saw in a prairie a great herd of buffalos.... They fired several volleys and shot off an extraordinary number of arrows.... More than 1200 buffalos were killed during our hunt, without counting the bears, does, stags, bucks, young turkeys, and lynxes.

The Appearance of the Illinois

They are tattooed behind from the shoulders to the heels, and as soon as they have reached the age of twenty-five, on the front of the stomach, the sides, and the upper arms.

The Customs of the Illinois

Formerly a man had to make several attacks on the enemy before he could marry... so that they were really about thirty when they married. The girls also waited till they were twenty-five. At present there are men who do not wait till they are twenty, and girls marry under eighteen. The old men say that the French have corrupted them.

The Games of the Illinois

Before they set out for the chase, the men play at Lacrosse, [all six Indian villages at Pimetoui].... They place in the middle of the prairie, on whose edge their village stands, two forks about ten paces apart. An old man, who is neutral, rises and utters a cry which signifies: It is time. Everybody rises and utters cries similar to those they utter when they attack the enemy. The old man throws the ball into the air and pell-mell they all try to catch it.

Treatment of the Dead

After this they take measures to procure for them, so the old men say, passage over a great river, on whose nearer shore they hear delights. There, they say, they always dance, and they eat everything they wish. The women there are always beautiful, and it is never cold.

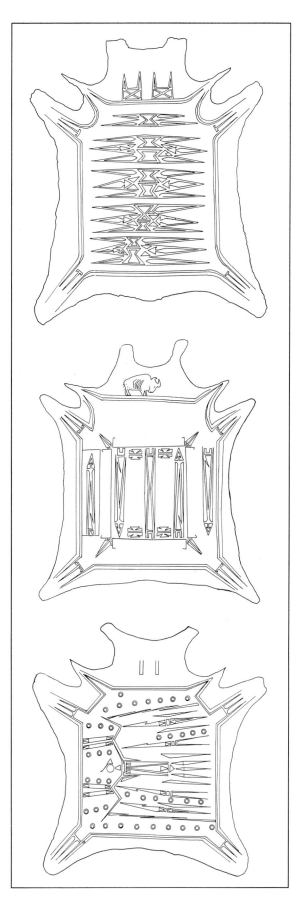

Painted hides from the Illinois Country, which decorated the ceiling of the principal gallery of the old cabinet of Louis XV in 1768. Museé de l'Homme, Paris.

Fort St. Louis (Old Fort and Village) —
1691 to 1763

The fort that Tonti and his men built in the winter of 1691–1692 at Lake Pimetoui was surrounded by 1,800 pickets. It enclosed two large log buildings — one a lodging and the other a warehouse — and two houses built of uprights for the soldiers. The trading concession was owned by Tonti, La Forest, and Accault and was managed during their frequent absences by Delliette.

At Peoria, six of the eight Illinois tribes, (the Kaskaskia, Peoria, Moingwena, Coiracoenentanon, Maroa, and Tapouaro), including about 800 warriors, occupied about 260 cabins in a village extending about 500 yards along the river.

Father Gravier built a chapel, "outside the fort, at a spot convenient for the Indians," and raised a 35-foot cross. Other priests associated with the mission in these early years were Fathers Rale, Bineteau, and Marest. By 1699 the chapel had been enlarged and a new chapel built at each end of the Indian village, which now extended for more than a mile along the river. In this year some 30 Kaskaskia families moved southwest to the Cahokia area. By 1702, the site had been basically abandoned by the official trading operations of the Tonti family and their associates, although Delliette was active in the area until 1719. Father Gravier left the mission for the last time in 1705 after he was attacked by one of the Peoria.

Reconstruction of Fort St. Louis, built by Tonti at Peoria in 1691. Illiniwek, Vol. 14, No. 1, 1976.

The years between 1704 and 1722 were a time of increasing hostility and warfare between the Illinois and the Kickapoo, Mascouten, and Fox, among others. Priests associated with the mission during these years were Fathers De Ville and De Kérében. In 1721 Father Charlevoix reported finding several hundred Indians and four French at Peoria. After a devastating attack by the Fox at Starved Rock in 1722, the Peoria, which included 600 to 700 warriors, moved south to join other Illinois tribes near Cahokia.

In 1733, after a ten-year interval, the Peoria returned to the Lake. During the next decades of serious hostility between tribal groups, the village of the Peoria continued to have contact with passing voyageurs, traders, missionaries, and the French government through its commandant at Fort de Chartres.

In 1750, there was a village of 1,200 Peoria at the lake, and a small Jesuit mission under Father Meurin. A Canadian trader named Descaris, at the request of the Peoria, built a fort for defense. In 1752 a party of Peoria chiefs and their families visited McCarty, the Commandant of Fort de Chartres to request a garrison. The officer Adamville and some soldiers were sent to Peoria. In August of that year, McCarty recorded what he had heard from Adamville:

> The Peoria stayed on their hunt only a very short time, the Sauk having warned them that the Chippewa were coming upon them five hundred in number; this leaves them dying of hunger: moreover as a result of the great drought they have little hope for the corn.

> The Chiefs gave him notice that they would take refuge in his fort if the enemy came. He tells me he is not in a situation to defend it, the fort being all decayed; for want of transport it is impossible to get it repaired by the voyageurs, the woods being a long way off. He cannot compel them, as it is impossible to have the pickets carried by two men over bad paths.

French control of the area continued to deteriorate, and the Peoria tribe had left the Peoria area permanently by the early 1750s, moving south to the Cahokia area. At the outbreak of the French and Indian War in 1756, the Illinois were allied with the French. The French traveler Bossu reported in that year that the Peoria lived in a fortified village on the edge of a little river. He probably found them at their winter encampment near modern Mauvaise Terre Creek, midway between Peoria and St. Louis.

In 1763, the French ceded the Illinois Country west of the Mississippi to the Spanish and the country east of the river — including Peoria — to the British.

●

Henri de Tonti, founder of Peoria, at Pimetoui, 1691–93. Lonnie Eugene Stewart; Peoria 1691 Foundation; Painted in 1990.

THE FRENCH AND INDIANS AT PEORIA — 1691 TO 1763

The French Villages at Peoria —1763 to 1846

The Old Fort and Village — 1763 to 1796

The years following the abandonment of Lake Peoria by the Peoria tribe saw the transition of Peoria from a seasonal Indian village with the intermittent presence of traders, priests, or military personnel to a small village of French farmer-trader inhabitants that lasted for about fifty years. Although the 1763 Treaty of Paris had established nominal British control east of the Mississippi River, continued Indian hostility such as Pontiac's rebellion and lack of cooperation from French inhabitants resulted in a relatively ineffective British presence at Fort de Chartres, and no British control upriver at Peoria.

In June of 1764, the Commandant at Fort de Chartres reported that a Potawatomi chief had forced the Peoria Indians — then encamped on the Mississippi River — to return horses and slaves which they had stolen from the French "habitants aux Piorias." Antoine Saint-François is said to have sowed corn in the area of the Old Fort and Village in 1763 and to have lived there until 1780. The British assigned Father Pierre Gibault to Illinois in 1768. He visited Peoria every other year until the American Revolution.

The earliest record of two of Peoria's most notable early residents is the sale by Jean-Baptiste Maillet of 30 acres of land near the Old Fort to Jean-Baptiste Point Du Sable in March of 1773. In August of that year, traveler Patrick Kennedy wrote, "We got to the old Pioria [sic] Fort and village on the western shore of the River, and at the southern end of a lake called the Illinois Lake.... We found the stockades of this Pioria Fort destroyed by fire, but the houses standing. The summit on which the Fort stood commands a fine prospect of the country to the eastward and up the lake to the point, where the River comes in at the north end."

Location of French Sites at Peoria.

The small French settlement at the Old Fort was inhabited by up to 30 people at any given time for over 30 years until its abandonment in 1796. During most of this time there was another small French village along the lake, a little more than a mile to the southwest. The Old French Village was located near today's Detweiler Marina, in an area now bounded by Caroline, Monroe, and Hayward streets. A plan of the village, made in 1840 in conjunction with French land claims, shows the location of four streets and 12 individual properties.

Plan of Old Village

Old Peorias Fort and Village

DRAWN BY C. BERNARD HULSEBUS 1934

No.		
	3.	Gabrielle Latreille (C. Troge)
	4.	Gabriel Cerré
	5.	Gabriel Cerré
	6.	Louis Chatellereau
	16.	Pierre Lavassier
	17.	Pierre Lavassier
	21.	Gabrielle Latreille
	22.	Thomas Lusby
	23.	Thomas Lusby
	57.	Josephin Boucher
	58.	Josephin Boucher
	A.	LaPierre
	B.	J.B. Parente (ungranted)
	C.	François Novelle (Lonvan)

The names of more than 60 individuals who lived at the Old Fort and Village are known. Among the noteworthy residents were Pierre de Beuro (for whom Bureau County was named), Jean-Baptiste Point Du Sable, Jean-Baptiste Maillet, Louis Buisson, Louis Chatellereau, Pascal Cerré, and Augustine Fialteau (blacksmith). These men were frontiersmen living in a frontier town. The conflicts between French, Spanish, British, American, and Indian interests along this stretch of the Illinois resulted in little effective governmental jurisdiction.

Born:	Before 1750, in either Canada or Santo Domingo.
Parents:	French and African-American.
Education:	"Well-educated."
Married:	Catherine, a Potawatomi Indian. Two children.
Achievements:	Trader, farmer, businessman. Owned a house and farm of about 30 acres at Old Peoria Fort and Village (1773-83). First permanent settler at Chicago (1784-1800) where he owned a trading post and farm.
Died:	1818, St. Louis.

•
JEAN-BAPTISTE POINT DU SABLE

•
Du Sable.
Conjectural Portrait;
Peoria Historical Sociey.

There was a mission at Chicago as early as 1696 and La Salle, Tonti, and Delliette had used the area as a trading post even earlier, but the first "permanent" resident was Jean-Baptiste Point Du Sable who moved his trading and farming operations there in 1784 after living for ten years at Old Peoria Fort and Village.

The British Commandant at Mackinac described Du Sable as, "a handsome negro, well educated … but much in the French interest." Other contemporary descriptions say that, "he has many friends who give him a good character," and that he was "a large man, wealthy, and he drank freely."

In 1800, after operating the Chicago post for 20 years, Du Sable sold his holdings, which included nine buildings on the north bank of the Chicago River, to the Forsyth and Kinzie families.

A detailed inventory of Du Sable's possessions when he left Chicago included cattle, mules, hogs and chickens, a flour mill and bakehouse, workshop, dairy, smokehouse, poultry house, stable, and barn as well as a great many farm implements and tools. His house itself was 40 by 22 feet. Among its contents were a French walnut cabinet with four glass doors, mirrors, pictures, and vessels of wood, copper, pewter, tin, and iron.

Du Sable spent the last years of his life living with his grand-daughter in St. Charles, Missouri. He is buried there in the cemetery of St. Charles Boromeo Catholic Church.

LOUIS CHATELLEREAU

Born:	About 1740, New France.
Parents:	Unknown.
Education:	None.
Achievements:	Attested as a habitant at the Old Village at Peoria where he was a farmer and fur trader for 17 years from 1778 until his death. Enlisted in Spanish militia at St. Louis in 1780.
Died:	1795, on his lot at Old Peoria Village.

Detail of Record of Mortgage of Louis Chatellereau, 1792. Byron R. Lewis Historical Library, Vincennes University.

Louis Chatellereau was not an exceptionally noteworthy historical figure of early Peoria but was perhaps typical of the early French habitant. He is the only early Peoria resident for which we have original personal records that give us some insight into daily life. These consist of a property mortgage from 1792 and the probate of an estate in 1796. Both were filed at the county seat at Vincennes. From these documents we learn that in 1792 Chatellereau owned a house, a farm, and a mill at the Old Peoria Fort and Village as well as five horses, 25 horned animals (cows, heifers, and oxen), and an Indian slave named Pointe Sable. In this year Chatellereau mortgaged his property to pay Gabriel Cerré, a well-known St Louis fur trader, for merchandise to trade for deerskins. This document was written in the presence of "Mr. Jn. Baptiste Maillet, Commandant of the Poste des Pes."

Following Chatellereau's death three years later, a record was made of his movable property, which included:

Animals

Three horses; 6 yoke of oxen; 6 cows with calf; 2 more cows; 3 two-year-old bulls; 2 one-year-old bulls; 7 hogs, different ages.

Furniture

Table with drawer, bedstead and featherbed, cupboard.

Clothing

Two cloaks, of different kinds; 6 pairs of breeches; 3 cotton shirts; hunting shirt; green round jacket; sleeveless round jacket; 2 vests; girdle; pair of boots; razor case with razors.

Domestic Household items

Tin sugar box, 11 tin pans, 9 tin dishes, 5 wooden dishes, 11 pewter plates, copper chafing dish, frying pan, 2 large soup pots, liquor box, 3 pottery milk pots, tin cheese mold, 2 candlesticks, pewter basin, 1 large and 3 small tin kettles, 4 copper kettles, brass tea kettle, bearskin.

80 lb. tobacco; 500 lb. flour; 56 bushels wheat (from his property, since a payment for reaping is noted); 400 paling stakes; a Negro fellow.

Tools and Equipment

Small hand-screw(?), without spring; brass-cock; pair of compasses and boring iron; 2 spades; 7 axes?; 3 pick axes; 1 small pick axe for the use of carpenters (?); saw; 4 handsaws; whipsaw; 2 cooper's adzes; 2 chisels; 2 large augers and 1 small; 7 steelyards; 2 drawing knives; pair of small scales; scythe-hammer; 9 sickles, plus 10 old ones?; 2 scythes; funnel; 3 small hammers; 2 fans; 4 sifters; 4 old bags.

Net for sturgeon; gun with the horn; mold for big shot; mold for ball; parcel of old iron; plough without share; large cart; 2 small carts, mounted; 2 harness, 1 with a chain; pair of horse fetters; set of harness irons.

•

Summary of items in probate of estate of Louis Chatellereau. Byron R. Lewis Historical Library, Vincennes.

PAGE
39

The records of Louis Chatellereau are the most detailed we have from which to reconstruct daily life in late 18th Century Peoria. From them we know that he owned a 100- by 300-foot house lot in the Old Peoria Village and farmed a lot contiguous to and behind his house lot. He had cattle for milk and cheese and apparently bred the cattle, since he had a number of bulls. He raised hogs and had four yoke of oxen apparently for plowing or operating his grist mill; or he may have used his horses for these tasks. At his death, several Indians were paid to bring in the horses. It was the French custom to have palisade-type fencing around farms and house property and to allow stock to roam free. Chatellereau grew wheat, fished in the lake, hunted, and had a variety of tools for carpentry and other tasks. He had a number of garments and household utensils

but almost no furniture. He was active in trade, presumably buying merchandise from St. Louis and trading it to Indians for deerskins which were shipped downriver. At his death, he owed money to a number of "engagés" whom he may have employed in trading operations. In 1792 he owned an Indian slave and in 1795 a black slave.

Chatellereau had a son who claimed his land after his death, but we have no record of a wife. Astonishingly however, we know that at the death of a good friend (presumably a Potawatomi), Chatellereau took into his home the man's three children — Gomo, Senachewine, and their sister — and raised them as French-speaking Catholics. Both Gomo and Senachewine were to become leaders of the Potawatomi.

The fortification at the Old Village was undoubtedly rebuilt many times over the years. The blockhouses were still visible in 1796, and fragments of burned pickets and heaped earth were reportedly noted in 1826 by property owner John Birket, about 150 feet above the Peoria Pottery. The last fort apparently stood just northwest of Adams street between Cornhill and Mary streets. By 1933 the site of the fort was an abandoned stone and gravel pit.

Chicago in 1820, viewed from Lake Michigan. Fort Dearborn is at the left (south of the Chicago River), and the Kinzie house and trading post property which were once Du Sable's are at the right (north of the river). Chicago Historical Society.

Jean-Baptiste Maillet
and the American Revolution

Born:	Before 1753, St. Denis, Québec.
Parents:	Augustin and Marie Madeleine Ebert Maillet.
Education:	Unknown. Probably illiterate.
Married:	Wife's name unknown. Son Hypolyte born 1778.
Achievements:	Trader. Founded New Fort and Village at Peoria in 1778. Appointed post commander at Peoria under Spanish allies of the Americans in 1779. Probably joined Spanish-led expedition against St. Joseph during American Revolution.
Died:	1801. Shot at Peoria by a man named Senegal (Senecal?).

Maillet [signature]

One of the most important of the early residents of French Peoria was Jean-Baptiste Maillet. For a period of about 30 years, during which the political fortunes of the town fluctuated wildly, Maillet seems always to have remained — either officially or unofficially — as the man in charge. A few facts about his life are known, and a number of stories have survived, some of which are clearly untrue. He was an individual to whom legends became attached.

In 1773, when the area was officially British, Maillet sold property at the Old Peoria village to Point Du Sable. The American Revolution, which began in 1775, at first had little effect on this frontier town but Peoria eventually became involved in a number of military campaigns. At times during the Revolution, Peoria was deserted by its inhabitants because of the danger of Indian attack. Although distant from the centers of power, Peoria was touched by the major political events of the time because of its location on a major waterway.

In January 1778 nine French inhabitants of Peoria wrote the British Commandant at Fort de Chartres that they had witnessed the arrival of his letter to Maillet in which the commandant had asked him to deliver a message to the Mascouten Chiefs. The French assured the British Commandant of their continued support. In July of that year, however, Col. George Rogers Clark, with 175 Virginia volunteers, took the town of Kaskaskia from the British and shortly afterward secured Cahokia and Vincennes for the Americans. He informed the French at Peoria that the Americans were in control of the region and that France was now allied with the Americans against the British. The messengers were two

He was of a strange composition and had a strong, uncultivated mind; but a great preponderance of courage and savage combativeness. (Governor Reynolds, writing from hearsay fifty years after Maillet's death)

PAGE
41

Frenchmen and three soldiers, including Nicholas Smith, who is reported to have said that Peoria was, "a large town, built along the beach of the lake, with narrow, unpaved streets, and houses constructed of wood."

In 1778 Maillet had established a new village at Peoria, a mile and a half southwest of the Old Village. Here he built a fortified house on Lot 7 (between today's Harrison and East Franklin streets). His son Hypolyte was born there that year. Late in 1778 Clark sent a company of forty men under Captain Linctot up the Illinois to secure the neutrality of the Indians and to distract the British from his planned attack on Detroit. Linctot's party crossed overland from Peoria to join Clark for a projected attack on Detroit or St. Joseph, which in the end did not take place.

In 1779 the Spanish joined the American/French Alliance. In May of 1780, a force of 300 British and 900 Indians descended the Mississippi River, and unsuccessfully attacked St. Louis and Cahokia, retreating up the Mississippi and Illinois Rivers. In conjunction with this effort, an attack led by Charles-Gautier de Verville was apparently made on Peoria and the fort burned. In retaliation for the raids, Col. Clark sent an expedition of 350 Virginians, French, Spanish, and Indians under Col. John Montgomery against the Indian allies of the British on the Rock River. This force obtained provisions at Peoria on what were apparently exorbitant terms, as reflected in Col. Montgomery's attempts to receive reimbursement from Virginia four years later.

Later that year Maillet was assigned twelve Spanish militiamen by Cruzat, the Spanish Governor at St. Louis. He was made responsible for watching the movements of the British and gaining the friendship of the Indians along the Illinois.

In the summer, the French officer Augustin Mottin de La Balme appeared in the Illinois Country, perhaps under the auspices (officially or unofficially) of Washington and Lafayette. His task was to inspire the Illinois French to assist in winning the support of French Canadians to the American cause. He found the Illinois French supportive of his plans, which they were led to believe would restore an official French presence to the region. He found the French dissatisfied with Col. Clark and the Americans, whose presence they blamed for antagonizing the Potawatomi, Sauk, and Fox who were all supporters of the British.

La Balme raised a force of about 80 French and Indians in the Illinois Country for a projected assault on Detroit. In November, this force, flying the French flag, attacked the British post of Miami. They were defeated and La Balme was killed.

La Balme had also dispatched a detachment of 17 men from Cahokia under the command of Jean-Baptiste Hamelin against Fort St. Joseph. Reaching the poorly defended post in December, they took 22 prisoners and a quantity of trade goods and retreated toward Chicago. The British caught them there and most of the force were killed or captured.

I was ordered to go on an expedition to Opee [Peoria] one hundred and forty Leagues By orders from General Clark where I was obliged to purchase Botes & provision for three hundred and fifty men & could not Git them on Eny other tarms, you may think hard of the Bill Being so high [more than $3,000], But notwithstanding the Sum we were Constrained to eate our Horses on our Return after fasting five days.
(Col. Montgomery)

Almost immediately, a much larger expedition against Fort St. Joseph was mounted at St. Louis by Cruzat, under the command of Pouré. In January of 1781 Maillet reported on British activity to the north in a letter to Cruzat, that was apparently written from a post at "Mauvaise Terre" (near modern Naples), just before he and his 12 Spanish militiamen joined the Pouré expedition of Spanish, French, and Indians as it came up the river. The river was frozen north of Peoria, and it was necessary to travel overland from there. The force took the post at St. Joseph on February 12 without a shot and held it for just 24 hours (under the flag of Spain), before returning to St. Louis.

Maillet retained his detachment of troops under Cruzat at least until the end of 1782.

Detail of Maillet's letter to Cruzat, 1781. Bancroft Library, Berkeley, California.

Clark stubbornly retained his control of the Illinois Country through the remainder of the war. As a result the area was secured to the United States in the 1783 Treaty of Paris .

The New Fort and Village — 1778 to 1812

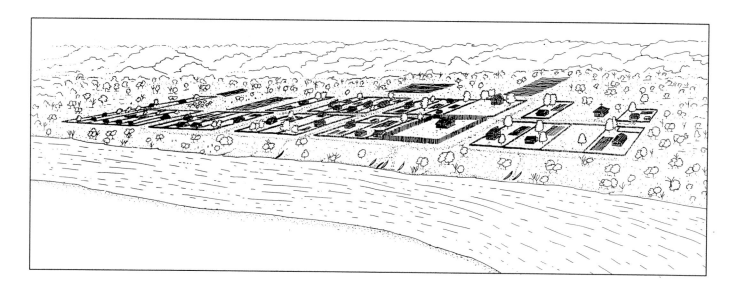

Reconstruction of the New Fort and Village at Peoria, 1778 to 1812. Dickson Mounds Museum.

Maillet apparently continued to serve as military commander at Peoria when it became part of the Northwest Territory and then part of the Territory of Indiana. He served processes at Peoria that were issued from the court at Cahokia. He received 800 acres at Peoria in three land grants, one of which was for military service. He was referred to as "Commandant of the Poste des Pes" in Chatellereau's mortgage document in 1792. After the 1792 (unratified) treaty of peace and friendship negotiated between the Potawatomi and French by General Putnam, both Gomo and Maillet reportedly traveled to see President Washington and were well received by him. In 1801, as the result of an "altercation," Maillet was shot at Peoria by a man named Senegal.

The new town founded in 1778 by Maillet on Lake Peoria, downstream from the Old Fort and Village, would eventually consist of some fifty buildings. The two Peoria villages existed beside one another along the lake for about 18 years.

The town had narrow unpaved streets, vertical-log houses surrounded by fences and gardens, and tilled fields outside the village. It was the custom of rural French to cluster their homes in villages apart from their (sometimes communal) farm fields. The inhabitants raised cattle, horses, pigs, and chickens. There were stockyards and barns, a winepress and underground vault for wine, a windmill for grinding grain, about six trading houses, and a church with a large wooden cross on the roof and gilt lettering over the door. There were blacksmiths, wagonmakers, carpenters, and shoemakers in the town. The names of about 100 of the inhabitants of the New Village are known. Among the noteworthy residents were Antoine Le Claire, one of the founders of Davenport, Iowa; Isaac Darneille, the second lawyer in Illinois; Antoine Deschamps; Michael La Croix; and Thomas Forsyth.

In 1806 Thomas Forsyth established the trading house of Kinzie, Forsyth & Co. Some 66 customers are listed in the company's ledger. Hypolyte Maillet, for example, bought calico, whiskey, candies, gunpowder, and corn and received a credit for 28 pounds of beef and a cowhide. Margeret Coursolle bought two snuffboxes and a pack of playing cards and is credited with 76 pounds of beef. Madame Raboin bought cotton, silk, sugar, chocolate, and ribbons and received credit for making 13 shirts.

The prominent American settler, Charles Balance, wrote of the remains of the destroyed French village in 1831:

> Some of the houses had posts in the ground and some were framed with sills... the spaces between the posts were filled with pieces of timber laid horizontally, with mud between them. The chimneys were made of mud and sticks.

In 1882, Matson described, from collected reminiscences, the long-departed French inhabitants of Peoria in "Pioneers of Illinois:"

> Their standard of morality was high.... They were a gay, happy people, having many social parties, wine suppers, balls and public festivals. They lived in harmony with the Indians, who were their neighbors and friends.... Although long since separated from civilized society, they retain much of the refinement and politeness so common to their race; and it is a remarkable fact that the roughest hunter or boatsman among them could appear in a ball-room or at a gay party with the ease and grace of a well-bred gentleman.

•
Typical French House of the Illinois Country. Collection of Pierre Choteau, St. Louis.

PAGE
45

However, in 1786 Father Pierre Gibault, who had been resident priest in the Illinois Country since 1768, wrote to his bishop from Kaskaskia:

> *In Canada all is civilized, here all is barbarous....*
> *Everybody is in poverty, which engenders theft and rapine.*
> *Wantonness and drunkenness pass here as elegance and amusements*
> *quite in style. Breaking of limbs, murder by means of a dagger, sabre,*
> *or sword are common, and pistols and guns are but toys in these*
> *regions.... No commandant, no troops, no prison, no hangman....*
> *I could name a great number of persons assassinated in all the villages*
> *of the region.*

The End of the French Villages

By the 1770s the Potawatomi had moved downriver to settle near Peoria. Lieutenant John Armstrong's expedition down the Illinois in 1790 records "a French trading Place" at Peoria. Armstrong states that "The position of this French post is indicated by small, rough roofs and appears to have been located on the west shore of Lake Peoria at its westernmost point. French villages were located on or near this site for many years."

The Old Peoria Fort and Village was finally abandoned in 1796 or 1797, leaving only the New Village occupied. In 1796 Father Levadoux said, "I arrived at pey-houryas, a little village about two leagues from the Illinois, and on the river of the same name. The village consists of about eighteen to twenty French families, all very poor."

The War of 1812 once again brought the Peoria French into the position of being technically Americans at war with the British and their allies, the Potawatomi. Since the Peoria French had a close association with the Potawatomi, who lived nearby and with whom they traded, their position was difficult.

In August of 1812, Fort Dearborn, the American post at Chicago, was taken by the Potawatomi, and many of the inhabitants were killed or taken prisoner. Thomas Forsyth of Peoria, half-brother and partner of the Chicago trader Kinzie, went north to negotiate with the Indians for the return of captives.

In October, Ninian Edwards, Governor of the Illinois Territory, led an attack of mounted troops against the Potawatomi village of Chief Black Partridge at the head of Peoria Lake. Twenty-five to thirty Indians were killed. Captain Thomas Craig of Shawneetown had been dispatched with his company and two boats to participate in the raid, but by the time they arrived at Peoria, the successful attacking force had already departed.

The events that followed are best reported by Ernest E. East's summary of Thomas Forsyth's account:

> Craig found that half of the Peoria French had fled to the southern settlements. His men looted vacant houses, including the warehouse of Thomas Forsyth, United States Indian sub-agent....

> Forsyth was absent when Craig came. He was returning by boat from St. Louis where he had gone with Lieutenant Linai T. Helm, whom he had ransomed from an Indian captor after the Fort Dearborn massacre. Forsyth, upon his return, demanded that Craig restore his goods and those of other inhabitants which had been removed to one of the commander's boats. Only a portion of the loot was returned by the troops. Indians in the night fired on Craig's boats, and the commander angrily accused the French of having knowledge of the Indians' intentions. This was denied. Craig then "arrested" the inhabitants. He set fire to four houses and to four barns, two of the latter containing wheat. He forced forty-one men, women, and children to enter two open boats in which he conducted them to

Festivities of the early French in Illinois. Henry Howe; "Historical Collections of the Great West," Cincinnati, 1851; the Newberry Library.

PAGE
47

THE FRENCH VILLAGES AT PEORIA — 1763 TO 1846

Savage's Ferry, near Alton. Forsyth was refused permission to leave men to care for two hundred head of cattle and other property. Governor Edwards ordered the release of the prisoners, but not until they had been held four days. (Journal of the Illinois State Historical Society, Vol. 42, No. 1, 1949, pp. 41–56.)

This incident effectively brought French Peoria to an end. In 1813 General Howard led an attack against Black Partridge and Gomo at Peoria. He built Fort Clark on the site of the burned French Village. The following year the Indians burned the fort.

Reconstruction of Fort Clark by Ralph Hubbard Peoria Journal Star.

The American government had not heard the last of the Peoria French when they deported them downriver in 1812. Several years after the incident, a number of the French petitioned the United States Congress for return of their land at Peoria which had been confiscated. The process of dealing with the claims moved very slowly and impeded development of downtown Peoria by the new residents. The detailed surveys of the French properties that were made to assist in settlement of the claims have provided valuable evidence for the history of French Peoria. Abraham Lincoln worked on some of these claims in the 1850s during his law career. The last of the claims was settled in 1867.

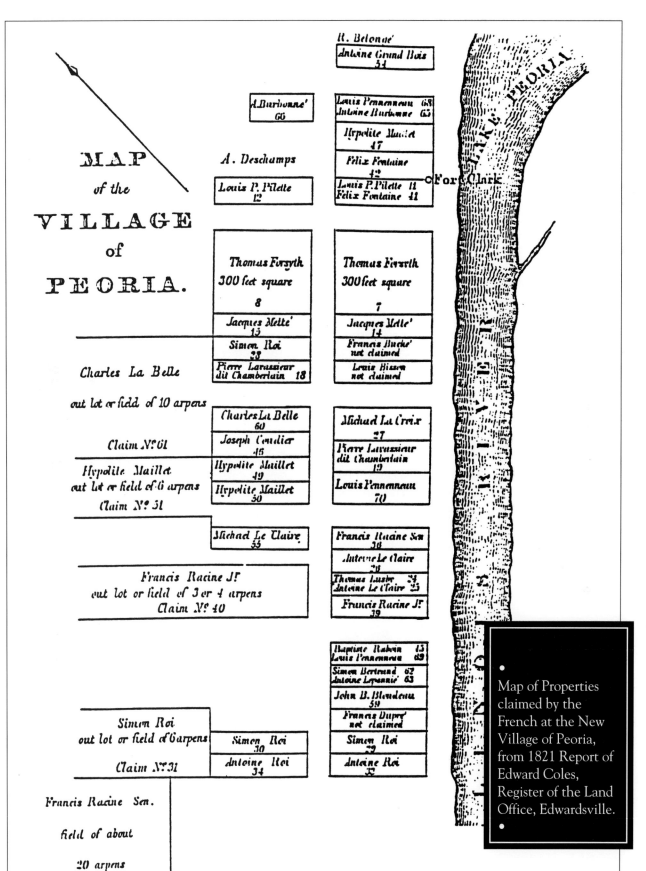

MAP
of the
VILLAGE
of
PEORIA.

R. Belonne'
Antoine Grand Bois
34

A. Burbonne'
66

Louis Pennenneau   68
Antoine Burbonne   65

Hypolite Maillet
47

A. Deschamps

Felix Fontaine
42

Louis P. Pilette
12

Louis P. Pilette   11
Felix Fontaine   41

oFort Clark

Thomas Forsyth
300 feet square
8

Thomas Forsyth
300 feet square
7

Jacques Mette'
15

Jacques Mette'
14

Simon Roi
28

Francis Buche'
not claimed

Charles La Belle

Pierre Lavassieur
dit Chamberlain   18

Louis Bisson
not claimed

out lot or field of 10 arpens

Charles La Belle
60

Michael La Croix
27

Claim No. 61

Joseph Caulier
46

Pierre Lavassieur
dit Chamberlain
19

Hypolite Maillet
out lot or field of 6 arpens
Claim No. 51

Hypolite Maillet
49

Hypolite Maillet
50

Louis Pennenneau
70

Michael Le Claire
55

Francis Racine Sen
56

Antoine Le Claire
29

Thomas Lusby   34
Antoine Le Claire   25

Francis Racine Jr.
out lot or field of 3 or 4 arpens
Claim No. 40

Francis Racine Jr.
39

Baptiste Rabrin   15
Louis Pennenneau   69

Simon Bertrand   62
Antoine Lepennie'   63

John B. Blondeau
59

Francis Dupre'
not claimed

Simon Roi
out lot or field of 6 arpens

Simon Roi
30

Simon Roi
29

Claim No. 31

Antoine Roi
34

Antoine Roi
35

Francis Racine Sen.

field of about

20 arpens

Map of Properties
claimed by the
French at the New
Village of Peoria,
from 1821 Report of
Edward Coles,
Register of the Land
Office, Edwardsville.

•

A D E L I N E
LaC R O I X C H A N D L E R

Born:	1805, French Trading Post, probably near Mauvaise Terre Creek.
Parents:	French Canadians from Québec. Father, Michael La Croix, trader and Indian Agent. Mother, Catherine Dubuque, who later married John Reynolds, Governor of Illinois.
Education:	Attended school in Kaskaskia.
Married:	Samuel B. Chandler, Cahokia, 1834. One daughter who died in infancy.
Died:	September 17, 1900, Belleville, Illinois.

Adeline La Croix was only six when she was taken from her home in Peoria with the other inhabitants. However, eighty-six years later, when interviewed by the *Peoria Journal*, the memories of her early life in Peoria were still clear in her mind. While she made no great impact on history, she came in contact with many of the significant people and events of her times. She lived in a log cabin in the French village of Peoria in her early years and died in the 20th Century, a prominent resident of Belleville, Illinois.

Her parents were French-Canadian. Her father was a fur trader and Indian Agent at Peoria and along the Illinois river. Her mother was the cousin of Julien Dubuque, after whom the town of Dubuque was named. Adeline remembered her father's trading post in Peoria — a two-story house and storehouse on Lot 27 in the French village. She recalled a visit by General William Clark before her sixth year:

> *I was deathly afraid of the Indians who were constantly coming and going at my father's store. I was also just as much frightened at the Americans, for I could not understand them as well as I could the Indians. General Clark came to our house, and there were as many as a score of Indians there at the time.... He gave me, oh! a number of bits of ribbons, all colors, and these ribbons I threw out to the Indians, who eagerly grasped them.... My mother said that I laughed and clapped my hands.*

Then in 1812 when she was six:

> *I remember the time when Captain Craig took all the French settlers aboard his boat and brought them to the woods below Alton.... The French settlers were on the best of terms with the Indians, and the Americans were not, and it was decided to break up the trading post and it was done by the total destruction of the buildings and taking all the settlers who could be caught down the river.*

Adeline then lived in the French settlement at Cahokia and for a time attended school at Kaskaskia. When she was 13 her mother married John Reynolds who became Governor of Illinois. At the age of 26 Adeline moved with her mother and stepfather to Belleville:

> *Here I entered the old pioneer society. Before that we had been very exclusive, as all the French creoles were, but here we associated with the best people, who were then making the political and commercial foundations of Illinois.*

Several years later she married Samuel B. Chandler, who had come west from Virginia to work in the Galena lead mines and had moved to Belleville to operate a dry goods store. He was active in politics, a director of the bank, and helped to organize the Agricultural Society. He died in 1871.

In 1841, the Chandlers built a house at 310 South Illinois Street in Belleville. Adeline still lived there almost sixty years later when she was interviewed by a reporter from the *Peoria Journal*. She spoke of her memories of the French village of Peoria and her encounters with General Clark, Lafayette, and many of the governors and statesmen of early Illinois.

Cahokia. Lithograph by Wild and Thomas, 1846.

MAP OF ~

LA VILLE DE MAILLET

AS SHOWN BY THE REPORT OF

EDWARD COLES

REGISTER OF THE LAND OFFICE

AT EDWARDSVILLE IN

1821

KEY:

STREET

· PRESENT CITY STREETS ·

CLAIMS TO LOTS
—o—

CHARLES LA BELLE
OUT-LOT OR FIELD OF
TEN ARPENS. CLAIM NO. 61
HYPOLITE MAILLET
OUT-LOT OR FIELD OF
SIX ARPENS. CLAIM NO. 51
FRANCIS RACINE, JR.
OUT-LOT OR FIELD OF
THREE OR FOUR ARPENS · 40
SIMON ROI. OUT-LOT OR
FIELD OF SIX ARPENS NO. 31
FRANCIS RACINE, SEN.
FIELD OF ABOUT TWENTY
ARPENS.

A. BURBONNE · · · · 66
A. DESCHAMPS
LOUIS P. PILETTE · · 12
THOMAS FORSYTHE
300 FEET SQUARE · 8
JACQUES METTE · · 15
SIMON ROI · · · · · 28
PIERRE LAVASSIEUR
DIT CHAMBERLAIN · 18
CHARLES LABELLE · 60
JOSEPH COUDIER · · 46
HYPOLITE MAILLET · 49
HYPOLITE MAILLET · 50
MICHAEL LE CLAIRE · 55
SIMON ROI · · · · · · 30
ANTOINE ROI · · · · 34

R BELONGE
A. GRAND BOIS · 54
LOUIS PENNENNEAU 68
ANTOINE BURBONNE · 65
HYPOLITE MAILLET · · 47
FELIX FONTAINE · · · 42
LOUIS P. PILETTE · · · 11
FELIX FONTAINE · · · 41
THOMAS FORSYTHE
300 FEET SQUARE · · 7
JACQUES METTE · · 14
FRANCIS BUCHE (NOT CLAIMED)
LOUIS BISSON (NOT CLAIMED)
MICHAEL LA CROIX · · 27
PIERRE LAVASSIEUR
DIT CHAMBERLAIN · · 19
LOUIS PENNENNEAU · · 70
FRANCIS RACINE, SEN. 36
ANTOINE LE CLAIRE · 26
THOMAS LUSBY · · · 24
ANTOINE LE CLAIRE · 25
FRANCIS RACINE, JR. · 39
BAPTISTE RABOIN · 45
LOUIS PENNENNEAU · 69
SIMON BERTRAND · 62
ANTOINE LEPANNIE · 63
JOHN B BLONDEAU · 59
FRANCIS DUPRE (NOT CLAIMED)
SIMON ROI · · · · · 29
ANTOINE ROI · · · · 33

DRAWN BY — E. BERNARD HULSEBUS — 1934

Map of properties claimed in New Village. Drawn by E. Bernard Hulsebus in 1934, based on 1821 Map of Edward Coles.

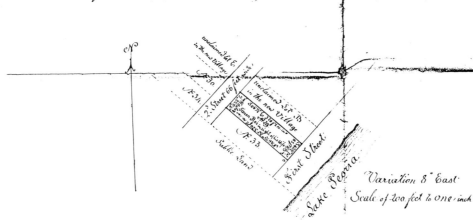

Record of award of Land Claim No. 29 in New Village to Simon Roi in 1823.

Peoria, August 29th, 1831. Lithograph by J. M. Roberts.

Note of Abraham Lincoln regarding Peoria French Land Claims, 1855.

The French Trading House — 1818 to 1846

Born:	About 1758, place unknown.
Parents:	Unknown.
Education:	None.
Married:	Potawatomi Indian, probably the sister-in-law of the trader Ouilmette (Wilmette).
Achievements:	Indian trader on Ohio, Mississippi, and Illinois Rivers for more than 50 years. Lived at Old and New Peoria Villages for about 35 years. Reported to have sided with the British in the War of 1812. Traded at Chicago. Established Trading House at Wesley City in 1818.
Died:	About 1830, probably at Trading House, Wesley City.

●

L O U I S   B U I S S O N

●

They were quiet, peaceable people, and treated the settlers with the greatest kindness, but these French traders cannot be classed as settlers ... they made no improvements; they cultivated no land; they established none of those bulwarks of civilization brought hither a half century ago by the sturdy pioneer. On the other hand, however, they associated with the natives; they adopted their ways, habits and customs; they intermarried and in every way, almost, became as one of them. (Chapman, History of Tazewell County, 1879)

●

Louis Buisson was one of a small group of French traders whose entire adult life was centered on the French town at Peoria. Shortly after the burning of the town in 1812, Buisson and another man were trading at Chicago where they ransomed a woman and child taken prisoner at the Fort Dearborn Massacre.

By 1818, Buisson and several other traders had returned to Peoria in the employ of the American Fur Company. Since the Americans were now established at the rebuilt Fort Clark on the site of the burned French village, Buisson established Trading House across the river, near the site of old Fort Crèvecoeur. About 30 Frenchmen and as many Indians occupied this settlement for about 25 years.

Buisson was described as "a large portly, gray-headed man"; his wife, "enormous in size (reportedly over 400 pounds), so fleshy she could scarcely walk"; and his daughter Mary was "greatly famed for her beauty and education ... obtained in a convent."

Mary often visited with my sisters at my father's cabin home, three miles southeast of Pekin. She was gay, sprightly, French in fashion and conduct, but spoke English well and was an agreeable associate with the young folks and finally married John Anderson of Tazewell County, but not of much character or face and she, his widow, left the country for the West after his death. (Letter of James Hainis, 1904)

The old French trading post was, "a long, log structure of … saplings split in two, set in the ground some 15 or 20 feet in height…. The roof was of long clapboards (cut in 3 foot lengths), and held in place by long heavy-weight poles of sapling trees…. held 3 feet apart by short braces." (James Hainis, 1904). Reconstruction of Trading House, Dickson Mounds Museum.

It should be noted that court records show that Mary was not widowed but divorced from John Anderson in 1836 on charges of cruelty and threats to her life.

Other notable residents of the post were Antoine Deschamps, Illinois Manager of the American Fur Co.; Antoine Bourbonnais; and François Bourbonnais Sr., and Jr., who were licensed to keep a tavern.

As new settlers moved into the area, the Trading House settlement declined. By the mid-1840s, the French traders and trappers, and the Indians with whom they associated, had scattered and moved west. The French Trading House was long remembered by the early farmers of Tazewell County .

The history of the Bourbonnais family is typical of that of many French traders who had become closely associated with the Indians. A number of these traders, including the Bourbonnais, were married to Potowatomi women. By 1834 the Bourbonnais family had settled along the Kankakee River. In 1836 they moved with the Potawatomi to land west of Missouri. When this became part of Missouri, the Potawatomi were moved to Iowa. In 1848 they were moved to Kansas. In 1872 the Bourbonnais family moved to Oklahoma where their log cabin still stands.

The occupants of the Trading House village were characteristic of the early occupants of our country — indolent, gay and not given to the business habits of morality, sobriety, and order. (Letter of A. Y. Davis, Tremont, 1904)

The Land the French Encountered

APPENDIX ONE

The French explorers made the earliest written records of what they saw around them — a land untouched by the influence of Europe. Their accounts of the plants, animals, and landscapes they found are of great interest and value to us today.

> *We have seen nothing like this river [the Illinois] ... for the fertility of the land, its prairies, woods, wild cattle, elk, deer, wildcats, bustards, swans, ducks, parrots, and even beaver; its many small lakes and rivers. That on which we sailed is wide, deep and still.*
> (Marquette Journal, 1673)

> *The country of the Illinois enjoys all advantages — not only beauty, but also a plentitude of all things needed to support human life.... The plain, which is watered by the river, is beautified by ... small hills ... covered with groves of oaks and walnut trees.... The fields are full of grass, growing very tall. That country is one of the most temperate in the world, so that whatever is grown there — whether herbs, roots, Indian corn or even wheat — thrives very well.*
> (Joutel Journal, 1684)

Bison from manuscript map of 1681. Bibliothèque Nationale, Paris.

> *We call them "wild cattle" because they are very similar to our domestic cattle. They are not longer, but are nearly as large again, and more corpulent. When our people killed one, three persons had much difficulty in moving it. The head is very large; the forehead is flat, and a foot and a half wide between the horns, which are exactly like those of our oxen, but black and much larger. Under the neck they have a sort of large dewlap, which hangs down; and on the back is a rather high hump. The whole of the head, the neck and a portion of the shoulders, are covered with a thick mane like that of horses; it forms a crest a foot long, which makes them hideous, and falling over their eyes, prevents them from seeing what is before them.*
> (Marquette Journal, 1673)

There is a species of wild cats called "pijoux," very numerous in these parts. These bear a great resemblance to ours, but are larger. I observed that some of them had very short tails, and others again much longer and thicker; they have likewise a very fierce look, and I have been informed they are very ravenous and good hunters. (Account of Charlevoix, 1721)

There are wood rats here as big as a French cat, which have white fur inclining to reddish, as long as that of a marten. It is very fine and the women make garters of it. They have tails a foot long and as thick as a finger, just like that of the muskrat. The female has two skins under her belly ... closed at the top and the bottom, and open in the middle. They have as many as eight young, which they carry inside when they walk. (Delliette Memoir, 1705)

There is also a great abundance of stinking animals, who produce an infectious stench with the smell of their urine. This is their defense; when one tries to approach them to kill them, they immediately turn tail and urinate if they can. The dogs, after having strangled them, are often like mad for a very long time. They do all they can by rolling on the ground to get rid of this bad smell. (Delliette Memoir, 1705)

Chat Sauvage

Rat de Bois

Bete puante

Drawings of wildcat, opossum, and skunk. Le Page Du Pratz. "The History of Lousiana," 1758.

Drawing of opossum. William Byrd, about 1738.

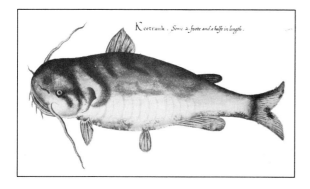

From time to time, we came
upon monstrous fish, one of which struck our
canoe with such violence that I thought it was a
great tree, about to break the canoe to pieces.
(Marquette Journal, 1673)

Watercolor of catfish.
John White, 1585.

There groweth also a certain
kind of Herb, whereof in Sommer they make
greate provision for all the yeare ... and only
men use of it, and first, they cause it to be
dryed in the Sunne, they weare it aboute their
necke wrapped in a little beastes skin ... they
put it in one of the endes of the sayd Cornet or
pipe ... and smoke so long that they fill their
bodies full of smoke, till that cometh out of their
mouths and nostrils, even as out of the Tonnel
of a chimney. (Jacques Cartier, 1580)

The tobacco plant. Pierre Rena and
M. de l'Obel, "Stirpium adversaria
nova"; London, 1570-1.

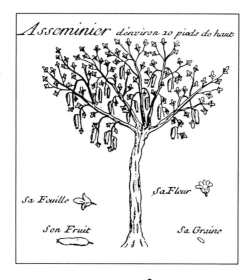

There are other trees as thick
as one's leg which bend under a yellowish fruit
of the shape and size of a medium-sized
cucumber, which the savages call "assemina."
The French have given it an impertinent name.
There are people who wouldn't like it but I find
it very good.... I ate, one day, sixty of them,
big and little. This fruit does not ripen until
October. (Delliette Memoir, 1705)

Drawing of pawpaw.
Le Page Du Pratz;
"The History of Louisiana," 1758.

The Fur Trade
in the Illinois Country

The North American fur trade obliged completely different cultures to meet and come to terms in order to obtain the goods they wanted.

The spectacular golden treasures taken from the natives of Central and South America by the Spanish in the 16th Century prompted other European adventurers and rulers to envision the New World as a source of fabulous wealth. When the French, British, and Dutch explored the great rivers and lakes of North America, they found a wealth of fur-bearing animals whose pelts were highly prized in Europe.

The struggle to control the lands where these animals lived and the American Indians who trapped them shaped events in North America for a hundred years.

In exchange for furs, Europeans gave the American Indians guns and ammunition; metal tools and weapons; cloth, blankets and clothing; glass beads and other trinkets; rum and brandy.

Within fifty years of the coming of the Europeans, the culture of the Indians of the Illinois Country was transformed. The native ways of hunting, farming, and fighting were greatly changed. The Indians' political and religious systems were radically altered by their involvement in conflict between the French and the British and their encounters with European missionaries.

Within 150 years, the Indians and the French traders were gone from Illinois, and the wealth of fur-bearing animals was greatly depleted.

•
*Trading transaction.
Cartouche from "Map of the Inhabited Part of Canada, from the French Surveys";
William Faden, 1777;
Public Archives of Canada.*

Control of the fur trade was a principal motive behind the initial ventures of the French explorers in the Illinois Country:

●

Fur Traders Descending the Missouri. George Caleb Bingham, 1845; oil on canvas; The Metropolitan Museum of Art, New York; Morris K. Jesup Fund, 1933.

• In 1673, the French government sent the fur trader Jolliet south from the Great Lakes to search for new trade routes and resources.

• The goal of La Salle's explorations was the discovery of a new water route to facilitate transport of furs.

• The posts at Chicago, Starved Rock, and Peoria were built as trading stations.

In the decade after 1682, the explorer Henri de Tonti and his cousin La Forest, with the assistance of Delliette and Accault, controlled trade in the Illinois Country from a French post at Starved Rock and thereafter from a post at Peoria. A small company of voyageurs plied the rivers between the Illinois Country and Canada, bearing European trade items south and furs north. Although trading seemed successful, governmental restrictions made it unprofitable, and in 1698 Tonti sold his rights to others and left the Illinois Country. Although the quality of furs from the Illinois Country was not equal to that of furs from farther north, trade in furs continued in the area throughout the French colonial period.

The beaver was the most highly prized of American fur-bearing animals. It was the staple raw material for the highest quality European men's hats. In 1738, beaver pelts constituted 60% of the value of furs taken from the Illinois

Country. Raccoon represented 14%, bear 9%, and deer 3%.

About 1700, the center of trading operations in the Illinois Country again shifted southward to the area where the towns of Kaskaskia, Cahokia, Ste. Genevieve, and St. Louis evolved. By the 1790s, the Chouteau and Menard families from these towns supervised trading operations along the Missouri River.

Beaver. Drawing from Baron de La Hontan, "New Voyages to North-America," 1703.

Although much of the Illinois Country fur trade eventually moved between Louisiana and Detroit via the Wabash River, small trading posts were maintained at Peoria during the 1700s to link southern posts with posts farther north.

After the French were removed from Peoria during the War of 1812 and "Americans" fortified and settled the west bank of the river, French traders working for the St. Louis branch of the American Fur Company returned to Peoria and operated the Trading House at Wesley City until about 1846.

PAGE
61

Beavers Building Their Hutts. 1760; "The World Displayed; or, a Curious Collection of Voyages and Travels"; Humanities Research Center, The Universtiy of Texas at Austin.

Buildings and Towns in the Illinois Country

The earliest settlements in the Illinois Country were on the upper Illinois River, but French settlement would eventually concentrate in the area where St. Louis is today. The major French settlements in the Illinois Country were:

1682 – Le Rocher (Starved Rock) — Fort St. Louis
1691 – Peoria — Fort St. Louis
1699 – Cahokia
1703 – Kaskaskia
1720 – Fort de Chartres
1732 – Prairie du Rocher
1750 – Ste. Genevieve
1764 – St. Louis

No French-period buildings are known to remain in the Peoria area today. The best preserved of the early French buildings of the Illinois Country today are all within 50 miles of St. Louis.

Court House, Cahokia, Illinois.
Built as a house in 1750. The
Illinois State Museum.

Reconstruction of the 1750
gateway of Fort de Chartres.
Dickson Mounds Museum.

Bequette-Ribault House. About 1785; Ste. Genevieve, Missouri; Photograph by Jack Boucher; Historic American Buildings Survey; Missouri Department of Natural Resources; Historic Preservation Program.

The Church of the Holy Family. 1799; Cahokia, Illinois; Cahokia Court House Museum.

Pierre Menard House. About 1800; Kaskaskia, Illinois; Illinois State Historical Society.

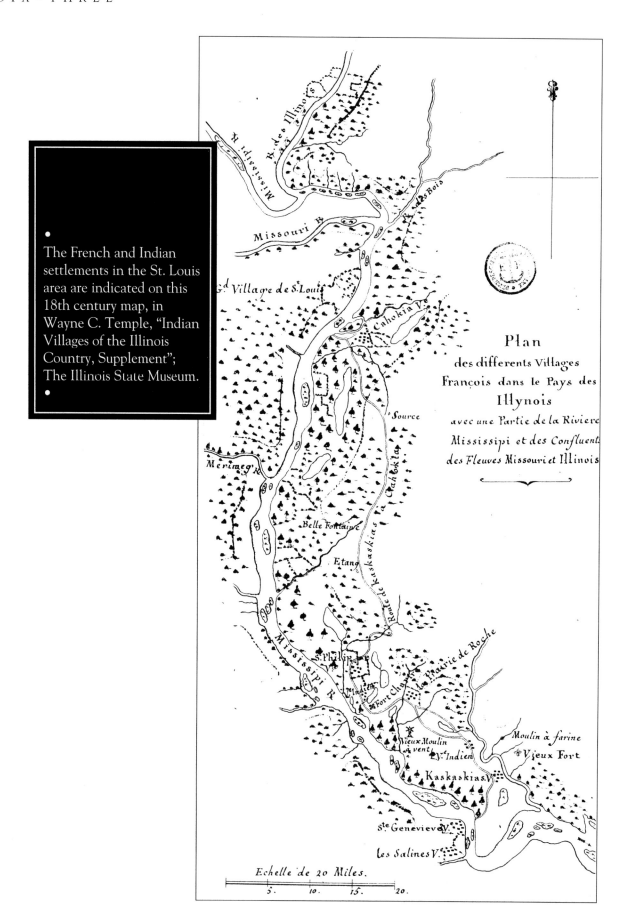

The French and Indian settlements in the St. Louis area are indicated on this 18th century map, in Wayne C. Temple, "Indian Villages of the Illinois Country, Supplement"; The Illinois State Museum.

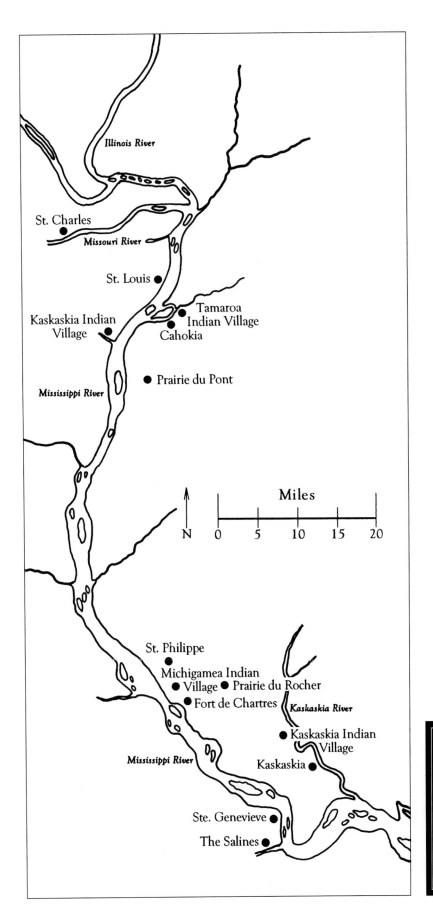

Illinois River

St. Charles

Missouri River

St. Louis

Tamaroa
Indian Village
Kaskaskia Indian
Village
Cahokia

● Prairie du Pont

Mississippi River

Miles

N 0   5   10   15   20

St. Philippe

Michigamea Indian
Village ● Prairie du Rocher
Fort de Chartres Kaskaskia River

Mississippi River

Kaskaskia Indian
Village

Kaskaskia

Ste. Genevieve

The Salines

●
French and Indian
Sites in the Lower
Illinois Country;
Dickson Mounds
Museum.
●

The Archaeological Evidence

The 1673 Peoria Village

As Jolliet and Marquette, the first Europeans to explore the Upper Mississippi, began to descend the river in 1673 in the area of what is now Wisconsin, Iowa, and Illinois, they encountered no people or settlements until June 25 when:

> *We perceived on the water's edge a somewhat beaten path leading to a fine prairie.... We followed the path and discovered a village on the bank of a river.... Four old men came out to speak to us.... I asked them who they were. They replied that they were the Illinois.* (Marquette's Journal)

The Frenchmen were welcomed at the village of some 300 longhouses with a feast and the next day were accompanied back to their canoes by about 600 people.

In 1993, 320 years later, this village of the Peoria tribe was identified through test excavations by the Missouri Division of State Parks. The site, in northeastern Missouri, had not been damaged by erosion or uncontrolled excavation and has been designated a state park.

A detail of Marquette's map indicates the Illinois River and "Kaskaskia," (Starved Rock) at the right, the Mississippi River at the center, and the location of the Peoria ("Pe8area") village at the left.

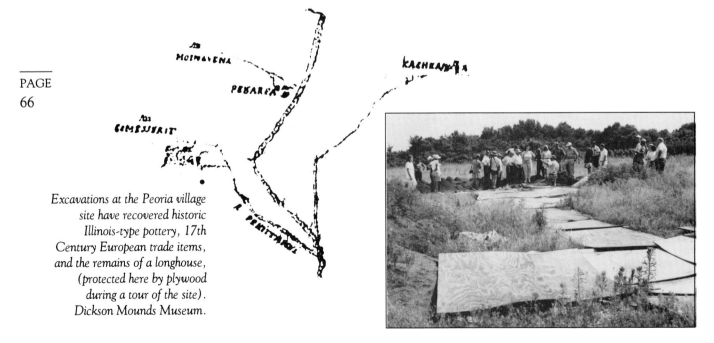

Excavations at the Peoria village site have recovered historic Illinois-type pottery, 17th Century European trade items, and the remains of a longhouse, (protected here by plywood during a tour of the site). Dickson Mounds Museum.

The Peoria Sites

There were undoubtedly many Indian settlements at Lake Peoria in the thousands of years that Indians occupied the Illinois River Valley. Although the general location of some French and Indian sites are known, not a single site or building dating to this long period has been documented by archaeologists at Lake Peoria. This lack of success is due primarily to the fact that remains of longhouses, campfires, storage pits, stockaded forts, and small wooden French structures did not make an imprint on the landscape significant enough to escape obliteration by 19th- and 20th-century urban construction. If remains of French or Indian occupation at Peoria are someday found, it will more likely be due to a lucky accident rather than to the result of a planned archaeological strategy.

Detail of "A New Map of the Western Parts of Virginia, Pennsylvania, Maryland, and North Carolina." Thomas Hutchins; London, 1778; The National Archives, Washington, D.C.

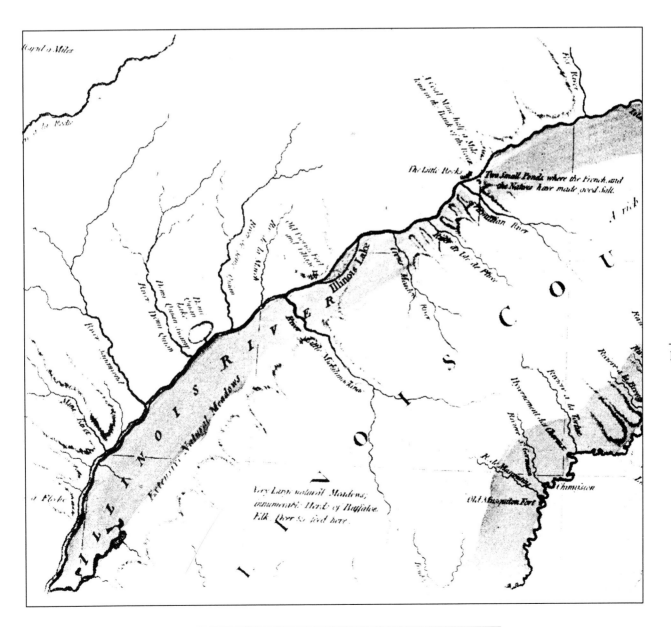

Excavations at Le Rocher

The French-period sites along the Illinois River that have provided the most evidence to archaeologists are those in the area of Starved Rock. These sites give archaeologists an extraordinary opportunity to compare descriptions by the French with the evidence of excavated material remains.

The French Fort at the Rock

When Jolliet and Marquette ascended the Illinois River in 1673, they found over a thousand Kaskaskia living near Starved Rock. In 1682 La Salle and Tonti built Fort St. Louis atop the spectacular landmark rock, which they called Le Rocher (The Rock). Shortly afterward, 20,000 Indians of the Shawnee, Miami, and Illinois tribes moved to the vicinity of the French outpost (see page 13).

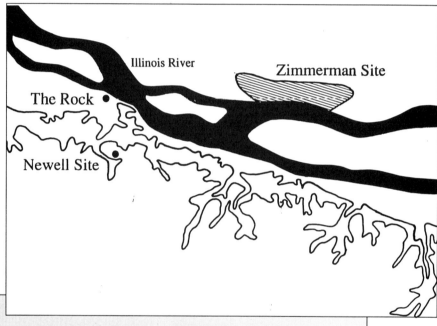

•

Location of sites at Starved Rock.

•

The Illinois River from Starved Rock, 1913. Bulletin 9, Illinois Natural History Survey.

Starved Rock.
The Illinois State Museum.

La Salle describes in detail both the Rock itself and the fort which he and Tonti built upon it:

> The fort is on the top of a rock which is steep on almost all sides, which the river washes at the foot.... It has a six-hundred foot circumference and is accessible from only one side ... which is closed by a palisade of white oak stakes eight to ten inches in diameter, and twenty-two feet in height, flanked by three redoubts made of squared beams.... The rest of ... the rock is surrounded by a similar palisade only fifteen feet high.... There is a parapet of large trees laid lengthwise one on the other to the height of two men, the whole being covered with earth.... At the foot of the fort there is a beautiful island cleared by the Illinois, and where I and my inhabitants have done our sowing within musket-range of the fort.

A 1687 account states that there was a large open area within the fort as well as several huts occupied by Indians, a warehouse or magazine, and a chapel. Partially buried remains of a fort were still visible when visited by Henry R. Schoolcraft in 1825.

In archaeological excavations on the Rock in 1947-50, 1974, and 1981, the most interesting feature found was a 16-foot-square cellar cut down to the surface of the rock and filled with burned debris which contained early French trade goods, gun parts and flints, and — most important — an embossed lead fur bale seal from the reign of Louis XIV.

Drawing of fur bale seal. Allan Ray Westover, "A History of the Archaeological Investigations at Starved Rock, Illinois."

THE ARCHAEOLOGICAL EVIDENCE

The Indian Villages

Since various tribal groups occupied the vicinity of the Rock over a period of years, there are remains of Indian villages at many places along the river. The largest area examined by archaeologists — called the Zimmerman Site — was the location of a number of Indian settlements between 1673 and 1722, probably including that known historically as the "Grand Village of the Kaskaskia."

Eleuation des Cabannes Sauvages

The La Salle expedition described the houses of this village as:

Long-shaped arbours, roofed with double mats of flat reeds, so well sewn together that neither the wind, nor the snow nor the rain ever penetrates them. Each hut holds four or five households and each household one or two families who all live together on good terms.

•

Iroquois longhouse. About 1720; Fort Frontenac; Detail from French map.

•

Plan of excavated longhouse. Oak Forest Site; Illinois. James A. Brown and Patricia O'Brien, "At the Edge of Prehistory."

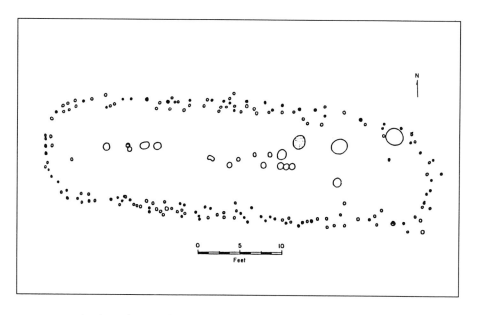

Archaeologists from the Illinois State Museum and the University of Chicago excavated the Zimmerman Site in 1947. They found postholes marking the location of houses of the historic tribes of the Illinois (similar to the complete house plan shown above excavated near Chicago).

● Excavations at the Zimmerman Site.
The Illinois State Museum.

Analysis of materials found in the excavations showed that bison provided more than half of the meat supply. The inhabitants grew corn, beans, squash, sunflower, and watermelon and gathered plums, hackberries, hawthorn fruit, hickory nuts, and walnuts. Found, in addition to the native stone tools and pottery, were brass ornaments, iron tools, glass beads, and other European trade items.

The Newell Fort

Due in part to the continuing raids of the Iroquois, Tonti abandoned Le Rocher in 1691 and established a post at Lake Peoria. Indians continued to regularly inhabit the area around the Rock, however, until at least the 1720s.

There was a French military post under the command of Delliette in the area from about 1716 to 1719. This post may have been on the Rock itself, or it may have been at the location known to archaeologists as the Newell Site.

On a bluff above a canyon behind the Rock are the remains of a fortified site which was operated by Jack Newell of Utica in the 1930s as an excavation to be viewed by tourists. Here a 250- by 350-foot area had been encircled by a trench. Around the outer limits of the enclosed space were 21 buildings which had been destroyed by fire. Almost all of the objects found in the excavations were European trade items or other European articles. There was also evidence of ironworking at the site. The character of the objects found is consistent with identification of the site as a French military or trading post dating to about 1711 to 1720, perhaps the post commanded by Delliette.

Plan of French Canyon site surveyed by Colonel Daniel Hitt. Rand, McNally & Co., 1877.

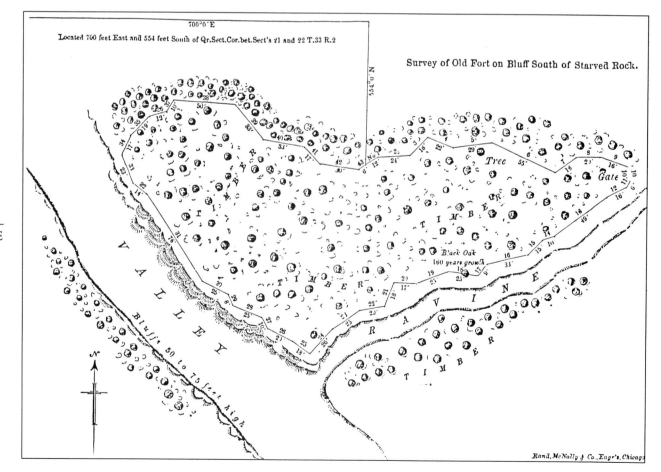

700°0'E

Located 760 feet East and 554 feet South of Qr.Sect.Cor.bet.Sect's 21 and 22 T.33 R.2

554'0'N

Survey of Old Fort on Bluff South of Starved Rock.

Tree

Gate

Black Oak
160 years growth

VALLEY

Bluff, 50 to 75 feet high

RAVINE

TIMBER

TIMBER

TIMBER

N

Rand, McNally & Co., Engr's, Chicago

The Mystery of Fort Crèvecoeur

The first structure built in the Midwest by Europeans, Fort Crèvecoeur, remains a mystery to this day.

When La Salle and his party of explorers came down the Illinois River in January of 1680, they found a large village of the Illinois Indians at Lake Peoria. Shortly afterward they built Fort Crèvecoeur and began construction of a forty-two-foot boat to take them downriver. When La Salle returned to Canada for supplies in March, he sent Michel Accault and Father Hennepin to explore the lower Illinois and upper Mississippi rivers and sent Tonti to determine the suitability of Starved Rock as a site for fortification.

In mid-March, nine of the twelve men remaining at Fort Crèvecoeur deserted the fort and supposedly left a written message saying, "Nous sommes tous des sauvages," ("We are all savages"). Tonti returned to the fort to salvage what he could and rescue the three men who remained. Just two months after construction of the fort began, it was abandoned and never reoccupied.

Fort Crèvecoeur. Based on drawings by Arthur Lagron, 1900s; Illinois State Historical Library.

Literally translated, "crève coeur" means "heartbreak." For many years it was believed that the fort was named to reflect La Salle's despair at the loss of his ship on the Great Lakes, the desertion of a number of his men, and the hardships of a winter expedition. It is now felt that La Salle's mood at this time was not one of despair. In France, "Crèvecoeur" was a family name, a place name, and the name of a military victory. It is likely that the fort was named after one of these.

Why Was it Called "Crèvecoeur"?

T H E   A R C H A E O L O G I C A L   E V I D E N C E

Where Was it Built?

The first mystery about the fort's location results from the fact that contemporary accounts of its site and construction are contradictory because they were originally inaccurate, were garbled in copying, or were edited for political reasons.

Father Hennepin's eyewitness account, although unreliable in part, does have a ring of truth in its description of the initial encounter with the Illinois at Peoria:

> *While crossing a little lake formed by the river, we observed smoke, which showed us that the Indians were cabined near there.... About nine o'clock in the morning, we saw on both sides of the river a number of dugout canoes, and about eighty cabins of Indians, who did not see our canoes, until we rounded a point, behind which the Islinois were camped within half a gun shot. We were in eight canoes, abreast, all our men arms in hand, and allowing ourselves to go with the current of the river.... The Sieur de La Salle was the first to leap ashore. (PL. IV)*

This description seems to indicate that the French found the Indian village at the place where Fort St. Louis was apparently later established on Lake Peoria, just below the narrows later called "Petit Détroit".

The location of this village is important, since La Salle and others indicate that Fort Crèvecoeur was built about three miles downstream from the Indian village and below the lake. In one account, La Salle says that it took him an hour to ascend from the fort to the lake by canoe because of ice in the river.

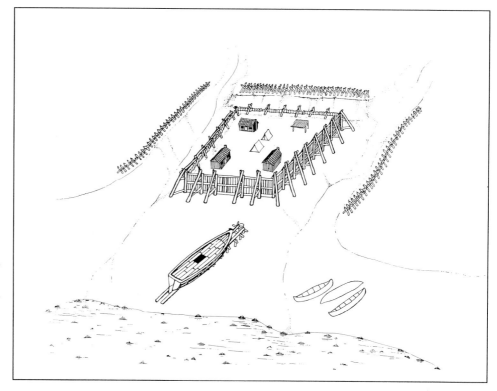

This reconstruction of Fort Crèvecoeur is based on La Salle's description. The fort was not a simple palisade of stakes since the "walls" of the fort held back the earth sides of the elevation on which it was built. Dickson Mounds Museum.

La Salle's own description of the site and the building of the fort is very detailed:

It was a little hillock about 540 feet from the bank of the river; up to the foot of the hillock the river expanded every time that there fell a heavy rain. Two wide and deep ravines shut in two other sides and one-half of the fourth, which I caused to be closed completely by a ditch joining the two ravines. I caused the outer edge of the ravines to be bordered with good "chevaux-de-frise," the slopes of the hillock to be cut down all around, and with the earth thus excavated I caused to be built on the top a parapet capable of covering a man, the whole covered from the foot of the hillock to the top of the parapet with long beams, the lower ends of which were in a groove between great pieces of wood which extended all around the foot of the elevation; and I caused the top of these beams to be fastened by other long cross-beams held in place by tenons and mortises with other pieces of wood that projected through the parapet.

In front of this work I caused to be planted, everywhere, some pointed stakes twenty-five feet high, one foot in diameter, driven three feet in the ground, pegged to the cross-beams that fastened the top of the beams and provided with a fraise at the top 2 1/2 feet long to prevent surprise.

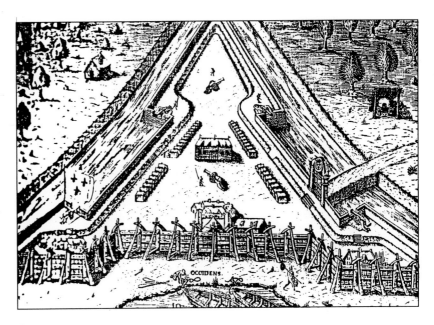

I did not change the shape of this plateau which, though irregular, was sufficiently well flanked against the savages. I caused two lodgments to be built for my men in two of the flanking angles in order that they be ready in case of attack; the middle was made of large pieces of musket-proof timber; in the third angle the forge, made of the same material, was placed along the curtain which faced the wood. The lodging of the Recollects [priests] was in the fourth angle, and I had my tent and that of the sieur de Tonti stationed in the center of the place.

The fort was, therefore, on an unwooded hillock less than 23 feet high, washed at its base by the river when it rained, and probably beyond the range of bullets or arrows which might be shot from the bluffs. Here the small group of men could build and guard their boat and launch it into the river.

PAGE
75

• The construction described by La Salle is similar to that of Fort Caroline, built by the French in 1564 on the coast of Florida. One wall of the Florida fort was a wooden construction which held back a nine-foot-high wall of sod. The engraving shown here was made from a drawing by Jacques le Moyne, who was at Fort Caroline in 1564. The Newberry Library.

What Became of the Fort?

For over a hundred years, historians and archaeologists have searched for the site of Fort Crèvecoeur. The terrain has been examined, old accounts and maps have been studied, and long-time inhabitants interviewed about local traditions. A number of individuals have devoted years in an attempt to discover either the remains of the fort or evidence of its location. At least seven sites have been proposed — all on the east bank of the Illinois River. In 1981 archaeologists examined these seven sites. They found no physical evidence of the fort itself and no artifacts dating to the time of the fort.

Of the sites proposed for Fort Crèvecoeur, the one that best fits the most reliable evidence was proposed in 1913 by Arthur Lagron, a French military and railroad engineer employed by the Peoria railways. Using the original accounts and old topographic maps, he concluded that only one location, at the edge of Wesley Slough, fits all of the evidence. (See Pl. XV.)

Proposed locations of the site of Fort Crèvecoeur.

Ghost of Fort Crevecoeur Slumbers Amid Roar of Rushing Railroad Trains, (Peoria Journal, September 4, 1933)

The "hillock" identified by Lagron as the probable site of Fort Crèvecoeur is indicated with a circle on this old topographic map. J. W. Woermann; Army Corps of Engineers; 1904.

A low sandy hillock on the Tazewell side of the Illinois river on what is now the right of way of the Lake Erie and Western Railway, 600 feet upstream from where the L. E. & W. joins the P. & P. U. to cross over the bridge into Peoria....When the L. E. & W. built their tracks right on the edge of that sand bank, they built one culvert for both ravines. (Arthur Lagron, 1933)

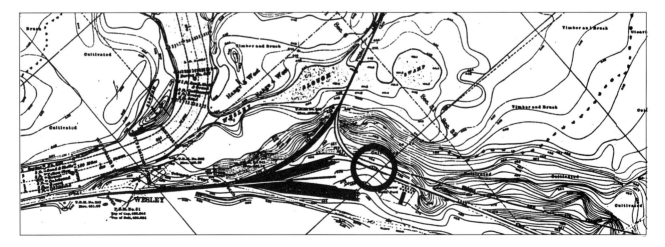

French Peoria on the
Map — 1673 to 1755

In 1673 the Illinois Country was unknown to Europeans. Only thirty years later it was a land regularly recorded by mapmakers around the world. European mapmakers, however, often had inadequate sources of information for frontier outposts, and mistakes or out-of-date information were often incorporated into newly made maps.

Both Jolliet and Marquette made maps to record their journey in 1673. Jolliet's map was lost when his canoe overturned on the return trip, but Marquette's original map survived. It indicates the course of the rivers the expedition followed and the location of the Indian villages they encountered, including that of the Peoria on the Mississippi River and the Kaskaskia at Starved Rock.

•

Detail of Marquette's original map of 1673. Archives de la Compagmie des Jésus; Saint-Jérôme, Québec.

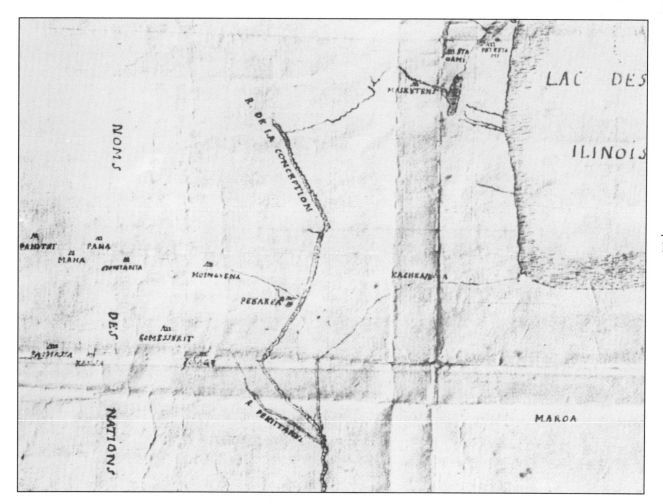

Claude Dablon, the head of the Jesuit Order in New France, based his 1681 map on information supplied by the Jolliet and Marquette expedition. It is the first map to name Lake Michigan, which is depicted at the lower right. The Gulf of Mexico is at the left.

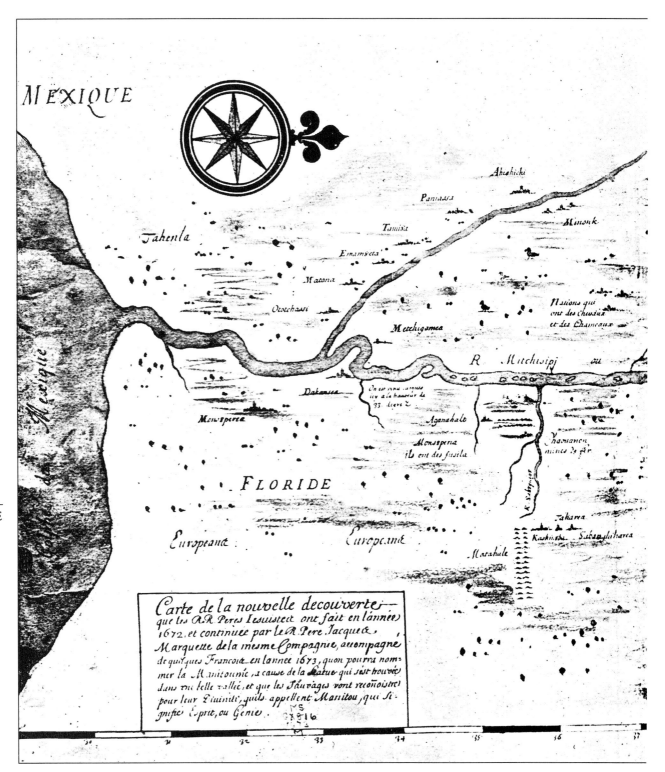

Manuscript map made to illustrate the
Jolliet and Marquette discoveries. Published in 1681;
Bibliothèque Nationale, Paris.

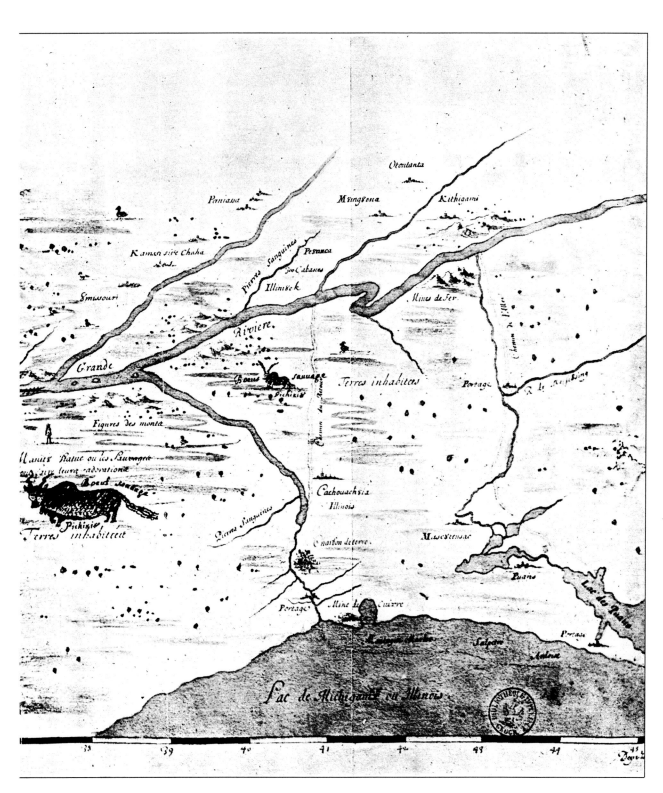

FRENCH PEORIA ON THE MAP · 1673 TO 1755

An early map made in France by the Abbé Bernou was based on information supplied by letters from La Salle (whose expedition descended the Illinois in 1680) and from a personal meeting in France with Duluth. The map records the location of the Indian villages near Starved Rock and the location of "Fort de Crèvecoeur," built in 1681 and already abandoned by 1682 when this map was made. Lake Peoria is also shown on the map. The Mississippi River stops abruptly just below the juncture with the Illinois because the full length of the river had not yet been explored.

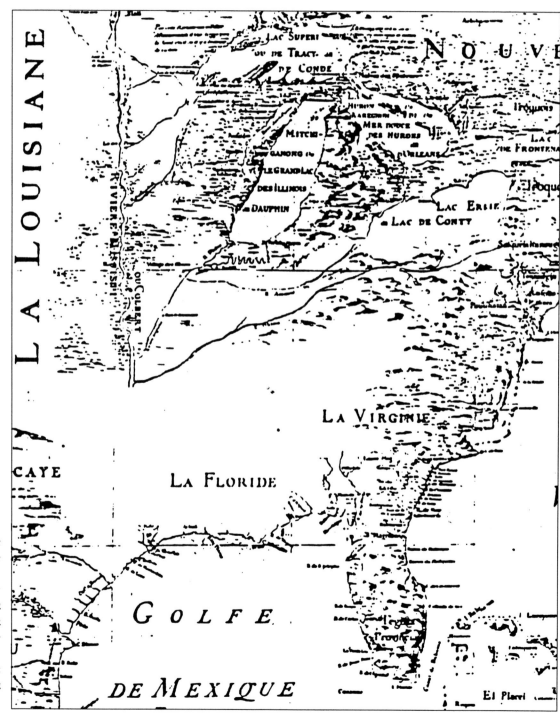

Detail of Carte de l'Amerique septentrionale ... avec les nouvelles découvertes de la Rivière Missisipi ou Colbert. Claude Bernou, 1682; Archive du Dépôt des Cartes et Plans de la Marine, Paris.

•

*Carte de l'Amerique
septentrionale … J. B. L. Franquelin,
1688; Service Historique de la
Marine, Paris.*

The well-known mapmaker, Franquelin, had an important
influence on mapmakers for twenty years. While the entire length of the
Mississippi — explored by La Salle to its mouth in 1682 — is shown on this
1688 map, the map reflects the incorrect course of the river reported by
La Salle, who placed the mouth of the river almost 500 miles too far to the west,
perhaps to facilitate funding for a new expedition. To accommodate this
inaccurate information, Franquelin has shown the river making a great sweep
westward, to enter the Gulf near Mexico. This error was incorporated in a number
of later maps.

This map continues to record the location of the abandoned Fort
Crèvecoeur at Lake Peoria (as did a number of later maps). It indicates correctly
the location of Fort Saint Louis at Starved Rock and records in detail the names
and populations of a number of the Indian tribes living there (see page 13).

A map made, probably in 1697, in Paris by Louis de la Porte de
Louvigny was based on information that he collected as an officer in New France
from 1690 to 1694, during the time that Tonti built and occupied Fort St. Louis at
Peoria. Louvigny's map labels the lake at Peoria ("Pimitoui") and labels the fort
— which it correctly shows on the west bank of the lake — the "Fort of the
French and Illinois Indians."

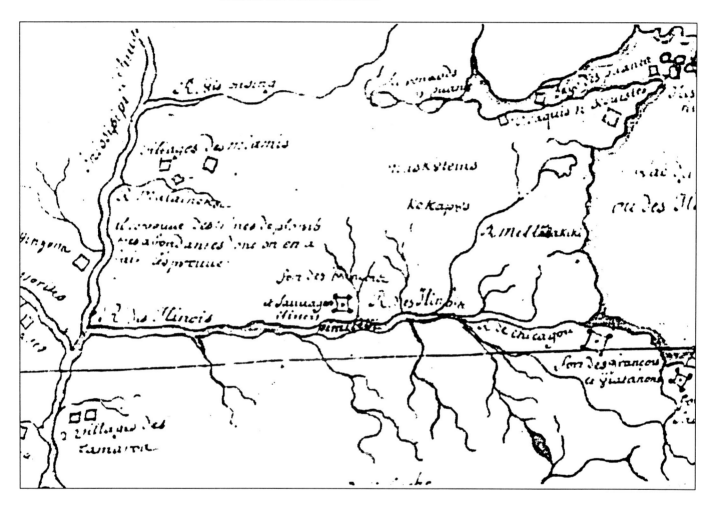

*Detail of Carte du Fleuve
Missisipi avec les Noms des
peuples que L'habitent.
… Louis da la Porte
de Louvigny, 1697, Paris;
Division of Maps, Library
of Congress; Washington
D.C.; Karpinski series.*

Delisle incorporated in his maps information that he collected
from many sources around the world. His 1703 map shows North America at the
height of French political power. The course of the Mississippi River is accurately
shown.

Delisle names Lake Pimetoui on this map but locates "Fort St.
Louis, previously called Fort Crèvecoeur," on the east side of the lake. In his 1718
version of this map, he shows no fort at the lake but indicates an Indian
settlement called "The Pimetoui or Peoria" on the east bank at the lower end of
the lake.

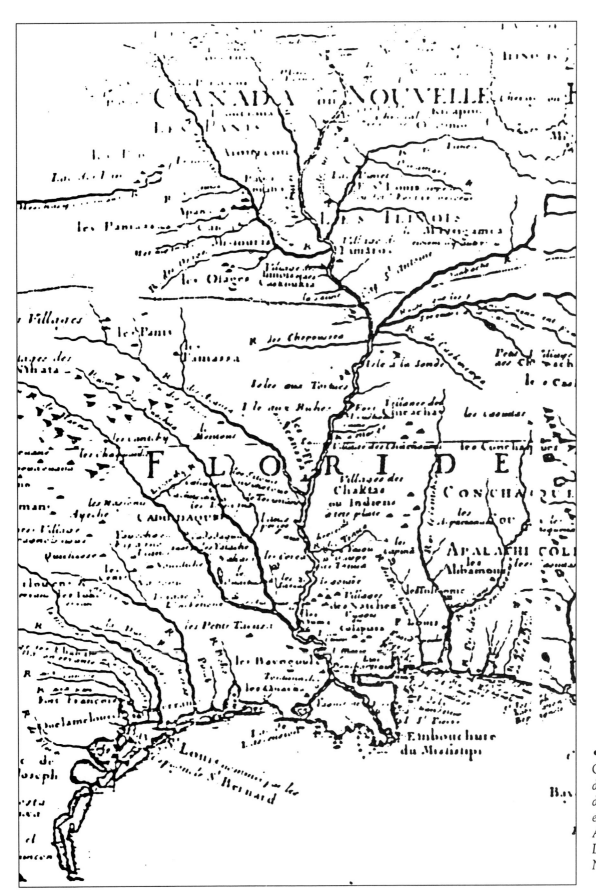

*Carte du Mexique et
de la Floride
des Terres Angloises
et des Isles
Antilles. Guillaume
Delisle, 1703; the
Newberry Library.*

Drawn at a time when the French empire in North America was coming to an end, Bellin's map correctly indicates the locations of The Rock, Lake Pimetoui, and the village of the Illinois on the west bank of the river.

Partie Occidentale de la Nouvelle France ou du Canada. J. N. Bellin, 1755; Historic Urban Plans; Ithaca, New York.

Thomas Hutchins was the first official geographer of the United States (commissioned in 1781). His 1778 map, a section of which is reproduced on page 67, shows the location of "Old Peoria Fort and Village" at the lower end of "Illinois Lake."

Events at French Peoria — 1673 to 1846

APPENDIX
SIX

In the mid-17th century, the Kaskaskia, Michigamea, Moingwena, Peoria, and Tamaroa were the primary tribes of the Illinois or Illini Confederacy which had recently been driven west of the Mississippi River by Iroquois attacks. By 1670, the Illinois were beginning to return to the east side of the river.

1673   Jolliet and Marquette encounter the Peoria in northeastern Missouri on their trip down the Mississippi River. Returning upstream on the Illinois, they find a village of the Kaskaskia tribe near Starved Rock (75 houses, 1,150 people). Marquette stays three days with the "Illinois of Peoria … on his return." He may have found them living at Lake Peoria.

1674 – 75   Marquette revisits the village of the Kaskaskia near Starved Rock where there are 1,500 warriors, 4,500 people, or 500 to 600 families. He establishes the Mission of the Immaculate Conception at the Rock.

1678   From April 27, Father Allouez is in charge of the mission at Starved Rock where there are now 8 tribes, 351 cabins, and 5,700 people. He erects a large cross in the village on May 3 and returns to Canada.

1679   La Salle's expedition comes downriver and arrives at Starved Rock in December to find the Indian village of 460 cabins deserted. He takes some of the Indians' stored corn for his men.

1680   La Salle arrives at an Indian village at Pimetoui (Lake Peoria). He builds Fort Crèvecoeur and a large boat. He returns to Fort Frontenac for supplies in March, sending Hennepin and Accault downstream and Tonti to Starved Rock. The men remaining at the fort desert in mid-March. Tonti returns to salvage what he can. In September Tonti and the Illinois tribes are attacked by the Iroquois at Starved Rock and driven out of the river valley.

1682   La Salle's reassembled expedition descends the Illinois and Mississippi rivers to the Gulf and returns upstream.

1682 – 83   La Salle and Tonti build Fort St. Louis at Starved Rock. Twenty-thouand Illinois, Shawnee, and Miami settle at four fortified Indian settlements nearby.

1684   The Iroquois attack Indian villages near Starved Rock.

1685 – 89   Tonti and La Forest administer the post at Fort St. Louis. The Indian confederacy disintegrates and most tribes move away.

1687   Some Kaskaskia are reported living at Peoria, but most are still at the Rock. Delliette arrives in October.

Joutel's journal reveals that in their retreat up the Mississippi River from the La Salle debacle in Texas, the party loses the main channel of the river south of Peoria and goes several miles first up the Spoon River and then up Quiver Lake before rejoining the channel.

1688   Delliette accompanies the Illinois on the summer buffalo hunt.

1689   Father Gravier, who later compiled a dictionary of the Illinois language, arrives in Illinois.

1691   Early in the year Fort St. Louis II is built at Peoria by Tonti and La Forest. The Mission of the Immaculate Conception is established by Gravier, one of four Frenchmen, including Delliette, there on May 10. Accault joins the trading partnership.

1692   Father Rale arrives at Peoria and finds 300 cabins in 11 villages. Delliette divides his time between the posts at Peoria and Chicago.

1693   The Kaskaskia and Peoria are living at four villages on Lake Peoria. Tonti goes to Québec. Rale leaves. Gravier builds a chapel and raises a large cross. Gravier's journal covers events at Peoria from March, 1693 to February 15, 1694.

1694   Gravier writes to France about the "scandalous" conduct of Delliette whom Tonti had left in charge at Peoria during the two years of his absence. Marie Rouensa and Michel Accault are married at Peoria. On April 11 Gravier and Delliette witness Tonti's report to Frontenac on the number of Iroquois killed or captured by the Illinois since 1687, (334 men and boys, 111 women and girls). Gravier leaves Peoria to go north.

1695   Tonti leaves Peoria for an extended trip to the Northwest.

1696   Father Bineteau arrrives at the Peoria Mission. Fort St. Louis becomes the only exception to the abolishment of all fur trading posts.

1698   Father Marest arrives at Peoria. Tonti, in Canada, cedes half of his trading share to his brother Alphonse. Tonti acts as guide to Saint-Cosme's party, which arrives at Peoria in November and encounters there Delliette, Marest, Bineteau, and Pinet. There is

Chief of an Illinois Tribe, Charles Becard de Granvelle, about 1700. New York Public Library; Astor, Lenox, and Tilden Foundations.

a chapel at either end of the village, apparently in addition to a church. On leaving the Peoria fort, Saint-Cosme's party is accompanied by Tonti as guide, and Bineteau, who travels as far as an Indian settlement near modern Naples. They break the ice for 400 feet to get out of Peoria Lake on their way south. They visit the cabin of Chief Rouensa on their first day's journey.

1699   Tonti sells the remainder of his trading concession to La Forest. Father Bineteau dies on Christmas Day.

1700   Father Gravier returns and moves south to River Des Pères near Cahokia with Marest and 30 Kaskaskia families to be closer to other Illinois tribes.

1701   Delliette goes to the Chicago post for four years.

1702   Violations of trade regulations result in abandonment of trade at Fort St. Louis. Tonti leaves Peoria for the last time and goes to Louisiana. Delliette and Alphonse Tonti continue trade from Chicago. Gravier returns to Peoria.

1703 – 11   Delliette remains the only French agent in the area but travels frequently.

1705   Gravier is attacked by a Peoria Indian. The blacksmith, Saint-Michel, is with him at the time. The Peoria mission is abandoned. Delliette, prohibited from trading at Chicago, writes his memoir in Montréal on the Illinois tribes.

A French Canadian of D'Ibervilles's force of 1697 prepared for winter warfare. La Potherie, "Histoire," 1722.

1707   Gravier reports from Paris that there are approximately 3,000 Indians at Peoria and 2,200 at Kaskaskia.

1710   Captain Joseph Kellogg finds the fort of the Peoria at Starved Rock, not at Peoria.

1711   In the spring, Marest, going upriver, passes through "the Village of the Peourias," 25 leagues from the Mississippi River. (It must at this time have been at Naples.) Coming downriver in midsummer, he stays with the Peoria at Starved Rock. De Ville is sent to the Peoria Mission and stays until 1714.

1711 – 22   The Illinois have two villages, one at Starved Rock and one at Peoria, during most of this period.

1712 – 15	Delliette acts on behalf of the Governor of New France to nullify British trade overtures to the Illinois and promote peace between the Illinois and the Miami.
1715	Delliette is given a sergeant and eight soldiers by New France to reestablish a fort (possibly the Newell Fort) at Starved Rock. He is probably associated with this post until 1720.
1717	The Illinois Country is annexed to Louisiana. A contract for trade between Delliette and Jean B. Dupre at "Illinois pimiteouy" is established.
	An anonymous French memoir states that at Starved Rock, "The Illinois [numbering 400 men] occupy the Rock on the bank of the river, and the French reside on the Rock which is very lofty and impregnable…. On this same river is an Illinois village called Pimytesouy, distant about fifty leagues or more from the Rock."
1718	Delliette acts for New France promoting peace between the Illinois and the Kickapoo, Mascouten, and Fox. Father De Kérében comes to the Peoria tribe. Boisbriant is appointed Governor of the Illinois Country by Louisiana. War with the Fox erupts in full force.
1719	The Fox attack the Peoria at Pimetoui and kill several women. The Peoria counterattack and take Fox prisoners which are redeemed by Delliette and De Kérében and returned to the Fox.
1720	De Kérében leaves the Peoria for the Michigamea.
1721	The Population of Illinois Indians is estimated at 800 to 900 at the Rock and Peoria. Charlevoix traveling downriver, finds four French and several hundred Indians at a village on the west bank near the lower end of the lake at Peoria.
1722	The Peoria settlement is abandoned as the Peoria join together at Starved Rock. Delisle on a trip upriver finds Peoria deserted.
1723	Renault is given a land grant at Peoria from the Company of the West.
1726 – 29	Charles-Henri-Joseph de Tonti, sieur Desliettes, (a son of Henri's brother Alphonse), is commandant at Fort de Chartres.
1729	In January, the Peoria winter at Naples, where Boucherville negotiates peace between the Illinois and the Kickapoo, resulting in a ceremonial meeting between the two groups at the village in March.

PAGE
88

"Canadian Trapper. St. Joseph,"
by Rudolf Friedrich Kurz,
August 8, 1849;
Kunstmuseum, Bern.

1730	In September, the Fox are massacred near today's Bloomington by French forces under Coulon de Villiers and Saint-Ange, assisted by Illinois, Kickapoo, Mascouten, and other tribes.
1733	Le Boullenger reports that (the year before?) "The Illinois who were among the Cahokias went to resettle at Pimiteoui. The others are at Starved Rock in more than 60 huts and are asking for Frenchmen and missionaries."
1736	There are 50 men at the Peoria village at the Rock.
1741	Peoria chief La Babiche takes Sauk prisoners from the Cahokia to return to the Sauk. The Peoria at Pimetoui send 60 men to attack the Sioux, but instead they attack the Fox at the mouth of the Wisconsin River. Returning down the Mississippi River, the Peoria are mistaken for hostiles by the Sauk who kill nine men. The Sauk apologize. Later, a party of 100 Sioux and Fox attack Pimetoui, but the village is warned by the Sauk, and only one Peoria Indian is killed.
1750	The Peoria are under heavy pressure from enemies to the north. There is a village of 1,200 Indians at Peoria and a small Jesuit mission under Father Meurin. Descaris, a Canadian trader, builds a fort at the request of the Peoria to control the "voyageurs." The Peoria kill a Potawatomi who is traveling through and ask the commandant of Fort de Chartres to intercede for them with the commandant at St. Joseph.
1751	The Peoria fort is assigned an officer and a small garrison by the French, to be maintained at the expense of the traders and "voyageurs" who pass through. The Peoria are attacked by Potawatomi, Mascouten, Menomini, and Chippewa and suffer heavy losses.
1752	In January, 21 Peoria chiefs are summoned by Commandant McCarty to Fort de Chartres. They bring their children and present calumets and gifts along with promises of allegiance to the French against the British. During the celebrations, Descaris sings a war song. Adamville is sent with soldiers to Peoria where they find the fort deteriorated. Adamville reports that the Peoria stayed on their summer hunt only a short time because of a threatened Chippewa attack and that they are dying of starvation.
1754	The Peoria are under attack by the Potawatomi, Kickapoo, Mascouten, and Sioux.
1755	At about this time, the Peoria leave Lake Pimetoui for the last time.

1756   The French and Indian War begins. The Illinois are allied with the French against the tribes to the north. In the winter, Bossu visits the Peoria in the lower Illinois Valley at a fortified village on the edge of a little river. He witnesses a ceremony honoring a new manitou (a spirit in the form of a goat-like creature) and tricks them into killing it and giving him the remains.

1757   The Peoria tribe has 700 warriors in the Naples area. There is a garrison under Toulan at Peoria.

1762 – 64   The Peoria, living in the area of Fort de Chartres, develop trading ties with the Spanish at St. Louis.

1763   The French relinquish the Illinois Country east of the Mississippi River to the British and west to the Spanish under the Treaty of Paris. The French garrison at Peoria under Toulon is withdrawn in December. Peoria is nominally British, but the French maintain a presence in the Illinois Country. The Jesuits are ordered out of Illinois, but Meurin, a Capuchin, returns.

Hamburgh's journal of a trip down the Illinois River states: "About 300 miles from St. Joseph is a french fort of very little importance. There was an officer and 5 men stationed there when I past it in the year.... From this fort or Port called Epic, it is 300 miles down the river [to] where it falls into the Mississippi River."

Early French Home in Illinois Valley. Victor Collot, "Voyage dans l'Amerique du Nord," Paris, 1826, the Newberry Library.

1764   Saint-Ange, Commandant at Fort de Chartres, writes to the commandant at Louisiana in June that the Potawatomi chief forced the Peoria — then encamped on the Mississippi River — to return horses and slaves that they had stolen from the French inhabitants at Peoria. This reference shows that by this date "Peoria" has become a place name that no longer refers specifically to the encampment of the Peoria tribe.

1765   Antoine Saint-François sows corn in the area of the Old Fort at Peoria.

1768   Father Gibault is assigned to Illinois by the British. He visits Peoria every other year until 1776.

A letter from Major General Gage to Forbes recommends establishing British posts at Vincennes and "Fort Dupice" (Peoria), to prevent French trade in the area.

1769	The Peoria hunt buffalo in the area of Starved Rock. (Last account of the Peoria in the upper Illinois River Valley.)
1770s	Potawatomi move down the Illinois River and settle north of the Old Fort and Village at Peoria. They later take the British side in the American Revolution.
1773	August 7, journal of Patrick Kennedy: "About 12 o'clock we got to the old *Pioria Fort* and village on the western shore of the River, and at the southern end of a lake called the *Illinois Lake....* We found the stockades of this *Pioria Fort* destroyed by fire, but the houses standing. The summit on which the Fort stood, commands a fine prospect of the country to the eastward, and up the lake to the point, where the River comes in at the north end.... To the westward are large meadows."
	Maillet sells 30 acres of land near the Old Peoria Fort and Village to Du Sable.
	The last reference is made to the Peoria in the Illinois River Valley at their wintering ground at Naples.
1775	The American Revolution begins in April.
1777	Trader Gabriel Cerré gives a deposition on April 29 that after having been at Peoria, he spent the past winter with the Kickapoo and Mascouten at Mauvaise Terre.
1778	In May, Rocheblave writes asking his superiors that he be assigned to the River of the Illinois "where there are only a few Canadians who do not litigate because they own nothing."
	On January 26, the inhabitants of Peoria write to Rocheblave (now the British commandant at Fort de Chartres), that they have witnessed the arrival of his letter to F. Maillet "and of your word to be carried by him to the Mascouten Chiefs." They assure Rocheblave of their continued support. The document is signed by Jyte Truteau, Joseph Venault, Louis Chatellerault, Lateau Hay, Louis Jauntetot, Eustache Lampert, Joseph Verinat, Amable Val, Bapte. Casterique. "Witness, at the Pees, the 26th January. Lionnais."
	The New Village of Peoria is established by Maillet downriver from the Old Fort and Village. A fortified house and other structures are built. The population between 1778 and 1795 is about 100, but the town was at times abandoned during the American Revolution because of Indian raids.

In July, Col. George Rogers Clark and 175 Virginia volunteers, take Kaskaskia from the British and shortly afterward secure Cahokia and Vincennes for the Americans. Clark informs the French at Peoria that the Americans now control the region and that France is now allied with the Americans against the British in the Revolution. Messengers (including Nicholas Smith) are reported to have said that Peoria was "a large town, built along the beach of the lake, with narrow, unpaved streets, and houses constructed of wood."

Late in the year, Linctot and 40 soldiers are sent by Clark up the Illinois to secure the neutrality of the Indians and to distract the British from his planned attack on Detroit. The party crosses overland from Peoria to join Clark for the proposed attack on Detroit or Fort St. Joseph which does not, in fact, take place.

The Spanish join the American/French Alliance.

1780

Although testimony given in later years states that the French inhabitants abandoned Peoria during the Revolution in 1780 and 1781, the town is the focus of much activity during these years.

In May, a large British and Indian force comes down the Mississippi River, unsuccessfully attacks St. Louis and Cahokia, and retreats up the Mississippi and Illinois rivers. An attack on Peoria is apparently made by Verville and the new fort is burned.

In retaliation, Clark sends an expedition of 350 Virginians, French, Spanish, and Indians under Col. John Montgomery against the Sauk and Fox allies of the British on the Rock River. This force obtains provisions at Peoria, including boats and horses.

In the fall, Maillet is assigned 12 Spanish militiamen by Cruzat, the Spanish Governor at St. Louis and given responsibility for watching movements of the British and gaining the friendship of the Indians along the Illinois. His base of operations may shift between Peoria and an encampment sometimes referred to as "Mauvaise Terre," located near modern Naples. Montgomery is placed in command in Illinois when Clark goes to Ohio.

In the summer, La Balme appears in the Illinois Country to rouse the French settlers in support of the American cause in the Revolution. He finds that the French inhabitants are generally antagonistic to Col. Clark and the Americans. La Balme is defeated and killed leading an attack by a force of about 80 Illinois French and Indians against the British post of Miami (modern Fort Wayne).

La Balme had previously dispatched a detachment of 17 men from Cahokia under the command of Jean-Baptiste Hamelin against

Fort St. Joseph. Reaching the poorly defended post in December, they take 22 prisoners and a quantity of trade goods, and retreat toward Chicago. The British catch them there and most are killed or captured.

1781   Another expedition against Fort St. Joseph is mounted at St. Louis by Cruzat and commanded by Pouré. In January, Maillet reports on British activity to the north in a letter to Cruzat, apparently written from Mauvaise Terre. Immediately afterward, Maillet and his 12 Spanish militiamen join the Pouré expedition as they ascend the Illinois. They find the river frozen north of Peoria and travel overland from there to Fort St. Joseph, which they take on February 12 without a shot, with a force of 65 Spanish militiamen and the help of about 100 Potawatomi. They hold the post for 24 hours, under the flag of Spain, before returning to St. Louis.

1782   Cruzat maintains Maillet's troops until this year.

1783   Clark retains control of the Illinois Country through the remainder of the Revolution. The area is secured to the United States in the Treaty of Paris of 1783. With the Revolution over, settlers return to both settlements at Peoria. Maillet apparently continues to function as commandant at Peoria until his death in 1801.

•

French windmill of the early 18th century. Iliniwek; Vol. 12, No. 3, 1973.

1788   A number of settlers of French Peoria receive land grants under an act of Congress (Appendix VII).

1789   The French Revolution seems to have no effect on events at Peoria.

1790   The Potawatomi are established at Peoria.

Lt. John Armstrong's expedition records: "A French trading Place. The position of this French post is indicated by small, rough roofs and appears to have been located on the west shore of Lake Peoria at its westernmost point. French villages were located on or near this site for many years."

In March, Governor Saint Clair sends a message to a Mr. May (Maillet) "who resided at a small village on the Illinois River, commonly called Au Pe, the place where the Peoria Fort stood, where there are five or six French families.... [Maillet] had been appointed commandant of that place by Col. Clark, and ... is a person of influence among the savages."

On May 17, trader Hugh Heward comes down the Illinois and mentions two French settlements at "Lake depiorias." At the entrance to the lower lake is the narrows "petite Etroit." On the west side of the lower lake "is settled one of the name of Chattlerou." At the village "at the South Side of this small Lake are nine French settled among the Indians: Augustin Fecto, J. Bt. Amelin, Lapierre a Smith, Capt Mye, Deneau, & Miney & Parrant & Oullet Engages, & Disson."

1792   Following the (unratified) treaty of peace and friendship negotiated between the Potawatomi and the French by General Putnam, Gomo and Maillet travel east to meet with President Washington.

1795   In the Treaty of Greenville, the Potawatomi cede to the United States "One piece six miles square at the Old Piorias fort and village, near the south end of the Illinois lake on said Illinois river."

1796   Letter of Father Levadoux: "On [June] 24th I arrived at pey-houryas, a little village about two leagues from the Illinois, and on the river of the same name. The village consists of about eighteen to twenty French families, all very poor. I remained there three days, said Mass every day, and preached the word of God. I heard a number of confessions, performed some marriages, and administered baptism to several children."

The Old Fort and Village at Peoria are abandoned by this date.

1800   Spain returns Louisiana and the Illinois Country west of the Mississippi River to France in the Treaty of San Ildefonso.

1803   The Louisiana Purchase is signed. France sells the territory west of the Mississippi River to the United States.

1806   Thomas Forsyth opens the trading house of Kinzie, Forsyth & Co. in Peoria.

1807   A number of Peoria residents file petitions with Congress to include Peoria in the Kaskaskia district in order to be granted land donations. Twenty-four individuals who claim residence in Peoria prior to 1783 sign the petition (Appendix VII). Their statement to Congress says "that this Village was established about the year 1730.... Being also a deposit of the furr-trade west of the lakes and north of the Illinois river; and being the yearly rendezvous of Several Nations of Indians."

1811   Captain Samuel Levering negotiates with chiefs at Peoria on behalf of Governor Ninian Edwards.

1812	The War of 1812 again brings the Peoria French into the position of being "Americans" at war with the British and their allies, the Potawatomi. Since the Peoria French live near the Potawatomi and trade with them, their position is difficult.

Forsyth warns of the threat of Potawatomi attack. In August the American post at Fort Dearborn, Chicago, is taken by the Potawatomi and many inhabitants are killed or taken prisoner. Forsyth goes north to assist with ransom of captives.

In October, Governor Ninian Edwards accompanies an attack of mounted Rangers against the Potawatomi village of Black Partridge near the head of Peoria Lake. About 30 Indians are killed. In November Captain Thomas Craig of Shawneetown arrives at Peoria with two boats to find that the troops have departed and that many of the Peoria French have fled. He loots houses and Forsyth's warehouse. Claiming that Indians fired on his boats, he burns a number of French houses and barns and takes 41 inhabitants downriver by boat to Alton.

1813   Brig. Gen. Benjamin Howard leads an attack against Black Partridge and Gomo at Peoria and builds a stockade (Fort Clark) at the former site of the New Village.

In December, former French Peoria residents petition Congress for reimbursement for losses suffered in the burning and eviction of 1812, beginning a lengthy process of testimony, surveys, and litigation. Thirteen cases go to the U. S. Supreme Court.

1814   Fort Clark is burned by Indians.

1818   Several of the deported French traders return and establish the settlement of Trading House — a post of the American Fur Company — at Wesley City (modern Creve Coeur). Illinois becomes a state, and "American" settlers move into the area.

1826   Fragments of burned pickets and heaped earth are noted by property owner John Birket at the site of the Old Fort, about 150 feet above the site of the later Peoria Pottery on the riverbank.

1831   Traces of burned Fort Clark are still visible.

1846   The last of the French remaining at Trading House move away.

1867   The last of the French land claims at Peoria are settled.

The Inhabitants
of French Peoria

In 1933 Ernest E. East published a pamphlet entitled, "The Inhabitants of Three French Villages at Peoria, Illinois," a directory compiled from his many years of research on the settlement's early history. Since only a hundred copies were printed, this work is not generally known to the public or even to scholars working on the French colonial period today. We are taking the opportunity, therefore, to reprint this valuable article here with permission from the East family.

East points out the difficulty he had in compiling this information from scattered and incomplete records and the problems of dealing with a variety of spellings, misspellings, and nicknames of a population which was mostly illiterate and transient. His list represents the results of many years of meticulous research and is reprinted here as it appeared in 1933, except that several of East's own corrections have been incorporated, (in italics). No attempt has been made to incorporate new information discovered since 1933 and that may appear elsewhere in this book.

The land grants noted in this pamphlet are those received by 24 residents of French Peoria under acts of Congress in 1788 and 1791. Some residents received 400 acres as heads of families, and some received 100 acres for military service. Maillet appears to have received grants under both acts, for a total of 900 acres.

The Inhabitants of Three French Villages at Peoria, Illinois.
Compiled by Ernest E. East, 1933.

Dwellers in Old Peoria — 1765 to 1796

Also called "Old Peorias Fort and Village." At or near site of Fort Saint Louis (Fort Pimiteoui) erected 1691 – 92 by Tonti and La Forest. (U.S. survey approved Sept. 20, 1840, shows village lay on west bank of the Illinois river in section 3, township 8 in range 8 east of the 4th P.M., beginning at a point slightly below Hayward street, thence N.E. to a point on N. Perry Ave. about 125 feet above Cornhill St., thence at right angles to a point near corner of Mary St. and N. Perry Ave., thence to a point 75 feet above intersection of alley and Caroline St. between N. Monroe St. and N. Madison Ave., thence to the Illinois river at point 100 feet above Caroline St.)

Note 1:   Known years of residence indicated thus: 1765 – 1780; –1782 means before 1782; 1784+ means after 1784; 1795(?) means year doubtful.

A

Amlin (Emelin ?) Jean B., –1783; 3 land claims confirmed, one for military service.

Arcoitte, Francois, 1782 – 1783+; petitioned Congress, 1807; 2 land grants.

Arundel, William, –1783; petitioned Congress, 1807; 2 land grants, 1 military; removed to Cahokia; St. Clair Co. clerk and recorder; died Kaskaskia, 1816.

B

Babo, Francis, military land grant.

Belhumer, Joseph, 1795 (?).

Bernard, Etienne, 1778 – 1785; 400 acre claim confirmed "near the River Coteneau (Kickapoo creek) within 3 miles of Pioria."

Beuro, Pierre de, store clerk 1776; trader at Bureau creek; slain 1790.

Biore, Louis, –1783; pet. Congress 1807; land grant.

Biore, Louis Junr., –1783; petitioned Congress 1807.

Boucher, Francis, 1795; died before 1820; 2 land grants, 1 military.

Boucher, Josephte, 1795; heir of Francis.

Brunette, Louis, –1782+; land grant.

Buisson, Louis, –1783; petitioned Congress, 1807; military land grant.

C

Chatelerean (Chatelereaux?) Louis, 1778; died 1795.

Chatellerean (Chatelereaux?) Louis Junr., –1795; petitioned Congress, 1807; he or father had horse-mill; 3 land grants, 1 military.

Chevalier, Pascal, 1780.

Cerre, Pascal, 1790 – 1795.

Chevery (Cherory, Chervry) Jean Baptiste, 1779 – 1783; petitioned Congress, 1807; land grant.

Chevery (Cherory, Chervry) Baptiste, Junr.; petitioned Congress, 1807.

Chorette, _____, 1795.

Chorette, Marie Josephte, nee Tieriereau, wife of Chorette.

Coinoi, Louis, 1780 – 1795.

D

Ducharne, Jacque, –1783; petitioned Congress, 1807.

Deschamps, Ante., –1783; petitioned Congress, 1807.

Diffon, _____. Seen at Petit Etroit (Little Detroit, the narrows) 1773.

Dineau, _____. Seen at Petit Etroit, 1773.

E   Emelin, John Baptiste.

F   Fiailteau, Augustine, 1789 – 1796; had blacksmith shop.
         Fecto, Augustin. Seen at Petit Etroit (Little Detroit, the narrows),
             1773.

G   Grandbois, Ante, –1783; petitioned Congress, 1807; military land
             grant.
         Graza, Baptiste, 1769 – 1780.

J   Jourdain, Jean, –1783; pet. Congress 1807; land grant.

L   La Bell, Antonio.
         Laframboise, Joseph, 1795; (one Joseph Laframboise was son of
             Francis Laframboise who died in Chicago, then Peoria Co.,
             April 26, 1830.)
         Landeau, Charles, 1790; military land grant.
         Lapattre, Joseph, 1789 – 1794.
         Lapierre, Francois, –1783; petitioned Congress, 1807.
         Laroach,_____, (7 years a resident).
         Lavassieur, dit Chamberlain, Pierre, 1794+; military land grant.
         Leframbroise, Joseph (probably same as Laframboise)
         Lonigo, Charlotte, 1780.
         Louvel, Michael, –1783; petitioned Congress, 1807.
         Lusby, Thomas, 1795.

M   Maillet, Jean Baptiste, settled before 1773; trader; sold land at
             "Old Peorias Fort" to Pointe Sable, March 13, 1773; founded
             new village 1 1/2 miles southward, probably about 1778.
         Mailliette, Theresa, widow of Cattenoir; sold house and lot 1798.
         Miney, _____. Seen at Petit Etroit (Little Detroit, the
             narrows), 1773.

N   Novelle (or Lovel), Francois, 1780 (?).

P   Parent, Jean Bte., 1780 – 1783; farmed near old fort; petitioned
             Congress, 1807; two land grants, one military.
         Parent, Jean Bte., Junr., –1783; petitoned Congress, 1807.
         Petit (alias Lalumiere), Louis; sold military grant to I. Darneille.
         Pettier, Jean Bpte., –1783; petitioned Congress, 1807.
         Pilette, Louis, –1783; military land grant.
         Pointe Sable (Pointstable, Point au Sable, de Sable, De Saible)
             Jean Baptiste 1773, perhaps earlier, to 1783, perhaps later;
             French mulatto, bought land March 13, 1773, from J. B.
             Maillet; sold to Isaac Darneille; removed to Chicago river;
             gained wealth as trader; retired about 1796; pet. Congress,
             1807; one land claim confirmed; one rejected by Kaskaskia
             commission, 1809; testimony that he cultivated land between

the old fort and the new settlement, 1780. *Died Aug. 28,
1818 at St. Charles, Mo.*

R   Rocque, Augustine, –1783; petitioned Congress, 1807;
         two land grants.
      Rochere, Francois, –1783; petitioned Congress, 1807.

S   Saint, Francis, Antoine, 1765 – 1780; sowed corn, 1765;
         died in S. Illinois.
      Saint John, _____ (Shoenberger?) 1780 – 1795.
      St. Cyr, Hyacinthe, 1780; witness, 1820.
      Shoenberger (alias St. Jean) Jean Baptiste, 400 acre grant near
         the old fort of Peoria confirmed on account of
         improvements.
      Sibinger, _____, 1781; lot owner.

T   Tieriereau,_____ (see Chorette).
      Trogue, Charlotte, (insane in 1820) widow Pierre, and daughter
         of Antoine Saint Francis.

V   Verbois, (alias Blondeaux) Pierre, –1783; petitioned
         Congress, 1807; military land grant.

Note 2:   Testimony indicates inhabitants of Old Peoria were forced to
remove in 1780 or 1781 on account of Indian depredations. They
returned after the peace of 1783. Old Peoria was abandoned
gradually in favor of La Ville De Maillet.

Note 3:   "Inhabitants of the Illinois and village of Peoria" in 1807
memorialized Congress to include Peoria in the Kaskaskia district
that they might avail themselves of the benefits of an act granting
land donations to settlers. Twenty-four signed petition which was
received by Congress Feb. 26, 1807. It seems likely some of the
signers lived at Cahokia or elsewhere in 1807, but had lived in
Old Peoria prior to 1783, proof of such residence being required
under the act. Peoria was included in consideration of claims by
the board at Kaskaskia. Nicholas Jarrott, then of Cahokia, also
signed petition, but proof is lacking he ever lived in Old Peoria.

Dwellers in the New Village — 1778 to 1812

Also called Au Pied du lac (at the foot of the lake) and its several
corrupted forms: Au Pay, Dupee, Dupice, Le Pe, Lee Pee, Opa,
Opea, Opee, Pay, Pays, Pe and Pees, and New Village of Peoria.

U.S. survey approved Sept. 20, 1840, shows village lay on west
bank of the Illinois river in section 9, township 8 north in range 8
east of the 4th P.M., beginning at a point 125 feet above Liberty
street and the river, thence northwestwardly to Washington

street, thence southwestwardly to Oak street, thence southeastwardly to Illinois River. Outlots or fields extended westwardly toward the bluffs and southwardly to Kickapoo Creek).

B   Bellanger, alias Belonge, Raphael, –1812.
Bertrand, Mary, wife of Simon, and widow of John Demonchelle.
Bertrand, Simon, 1799 – 1803+.
Binet, Louis, 1810 – 1812; lived lot 45.
Buisson (Bisson, Beesaw, Besong, Bissow, Besau, Beason, Bieson) Louis, – 1812.
Blondeau, Drezy, 1788 – 1806.
Blondeau, John Baptiste, 1793 – 1799.
Bourbonne, Antoine, 1801 – 1812.
Bruce, Elijah, – 1812.
Buche, Francis, 1809 – 1812; petitioned Congress, 1813; lived St. Louis, Mo., 1836.
Buche, Rev. Father Jacques.
Buche, Sarah, wife of Francis.

C   Casterique, Bpte., signed letter to Rocheblave Jan. 26, 1778.
Castion, Joseph, 1793 – 1794.
Champlaine, John Baptiste, 1802 – 1810.
Chatellerault, Louis; signed letter to Rocheblave Jan. 26, 1778.
Chorette, _____, 1800; lived on lot No. 39.
Cicare, Antoine, 1802; witness, 1820.
Condier, Joseph, 1796; rem. 1797 – 8; died before 1820.
Coursoll, Jean Marie, 1801+.
Coursoll, Michael, 1801.

D   Darneille, Isaac, b 1770; lawyer, second in Illinois; Pease says he eloped to Peoria with a Cahokia matron; McCulloch says he was "brilliant but profligate"; bought 800 acres from J.B. Maillet July 6, 1801; sold to William (Colonel ?) Russell Oct. 5, 1807; also sold to Russell land bought of Baptiste Pelletier (Pettier?), of Pierre Verbois, dit Blondereau, and of Jean Baptiste Pointe Sable; practiced in Cahokia court; died in Kentucky in 1830.
Defond, John Baptiste, 1805 – 1812; commissioned Aug. 8, 1811, captain 2nd Regt. (St. Clair Co.) Ill. Ter. militia; military land grant; died before 1820.
Defond, Louis, – 1812.
Defond, Madame, wife of John B.; married (2) Francis Racine, Jr.
Dejeney Joseph, 1809.
Demonchelle, John, died before 1803.
Demonchelle, Josephte, married (1) Louis LaBonshier; married (2) Hypolite Maillet.
Demonchelle, Mary, wife of John; m. (2), Simon Bertrand.

D – cont.   Deschamps, Antoine, 1778 – 1812; justice of peace, Indiana Ter. 1801; justice of peace St. Clair Co. Ill. Ter. 1809; Ill. River mgr. American Fur Co.
Dupre, Francis, –1799 – 1801.

F   Fontaine, Felix, 1806 – 1812; petitioned Congress, 1813; removed St. Louis; died after Jan. 8, 1835; probably married (2), Annex _____.
Fontaine, dit Carsereau, Josephte, wife of Felix.
Forsyth, Robert, son of Thomas; born lot No. 7; lived St. Louis; platted Forsyth's addition in Peoria (on Forsyth St.); bought and sold French claims; married Ann M. _____.
Forsyth, Thomas, 1806 – 1812; born Dec. 5, 1771, at Detroit of William; est. trading post at Ft. Dearborn with brother Robert and half-brother John Kinzie about 1802; removed to Peoria; allowed two land grants on Lake St. Clair, Michigan Ter., 1809; justice of peace Ill. Ter. Aug. 8, 1811; U.S. Indian agent, April 1, 1812; pet. Congress 1813, U.S. Indian agent at Fort. Armstrong (Rock Island) 1817 – 1830; died Oct. 23, 1833, near St. Louis; will, proved Nov. 1, named sons, Robert and Thomas, and daughter Mary; manuscripts in Missouri and Wisconsin historical collections. Forsyth, Mrs., wife of Thomas, nee LeMotte, born in Hagerstown, Maryland.

G   Grand Bois, Antoine, 1801+; died 1807 or 1808.
Grand Bois, Madame, wife of Antoine, –1806; died after 1807.
Grand Bois, Antoine, Junr., probably son of Antoine, removed to Co. of Kent, Upper Canada; removed to Wayne Co., Mich. 1837; married Sophia _____.
Grand Bois, Aspasia, daughter of Antoine (Sr.) married Blondeau; removed to Jo Daviess Co. Ill. Grand Bois, Constance, probably daughter of Antoine (Sr.) married to Vandrz; her heirs sold interest in claim to Antoine Grand Bois, Jr.
Graveline, Joseph, – 1788.
Guerrette, Joseph, petitioned Congress, 1813.
Gunoille, _____, – 1812.

J   Jauntetot, Louis; signed letter to Rocheblave, Jan. 26, 1778.
Jourdean, Francis, 1800 – 1802.

L   La Belle, Charles, – 1812; petitioned Congress 1813; died before 1820.
La Blond, _____, 1798 – 1799.
La Bonshier, Josette, nee Demonchelle, wife of Louis; married (2) Hypolite Maillet.
La Bonshier, Louis, 1794; died 1802 or 1803.

L – cont. La Bonshier, Magdeline, daughter of Louis; married (1) Joseph Touchette; married (2) Nicholas Gloden; lived St. Clair Co. 1836 – 1846.

Labosierre (LaBonshier?) Lewis, appointed justice of peace for the county of St. Clair, Indiana Ter., Oct. 29, 1801.

La Croix, Adeline, daughter of Micheal; married to Samuel B. Chandler.

La Croix, Catherine, wife of Michael and daughter or cousin of Julian Dubuque; married (2) John Reynolds (Governor Illinois 1831 – 1834.)

La Croix, Michael, 1808 – 1812; storekeeper and voyageur; served British army war of 1812; died insolvent before Nov. 21, 1848, in St. Clair Co.; left will.

La Croix, Julia Maria, daughter of Michael; married to Lewis Morris.

La Croix, Rene M., son of Michael, married Mary A. _____; lived St. Clair Co. 1848.

Lambert, Eustache; signed letter to Rocheblave Jan. 26, 1778.

La Pance, Antoine, 1811 – 1812; pet. Congress; 1813.

Lavassieur, Angelique, daughter of Pierre; married to Benjamin Roi; removed to LaFayette Co., Wis.

Le Claire, Antoine, 1809 – 1812; born Dec. 15, 1797, at St. Joseph (Mich.) of Francis Antoine and Indian squaw; petitoned Congress 1813; married 1820 at Peoria Marguerite Le Page, born 1802, died 1876; granddaughter of the Sauk chief, Acoqua; interpreter at Fort Armstrong 1818; among founders of Davenport, Ia; Le Claire, Ia., named for him; died Davenport Sept. 25, 1861.

Le Claire, Michael, 1801 – 1806.

Le Doux, Charles, 1793; died before 1799.

Le Doux, Madame, wife of Charles; married (2) 1799 Simon Roi.

Lionnais, _____; signed letter to Rocheblave, Jan. 26, 1778.

Lusby, Thomas, 1798 – 1802+.

M Maillet, F.; received letter from Rocheblave before Jan. 26, 1778.

Maillet (Maihet, Mayet, Mallet, Moillott) John (Jean) Baptiste, born perhaps at Mackinac; important trader; process server for Cahokia court, lived in stockade fort on lot Number seven (French claims) probably post commander under British; retained by Col. G. R. Clark and Gov. St. Clair as commander; may have accompanied expedition against British post at St. Joseph; awarded 800 acres in 3 grants, 1 for military service; killed 1801 probably in an affray with one Senegel who shot him; John Lyle, administrator.

Maillet, Hypolite, son of J. B., born in fort 1777 – 78; evicted 1812; lieut. 2nd Regt. St. Clair Co. Ill. Ter. militia; petitioned Congress 1813; died Cahokia, 1824, leaving 3 children, Hypolite; Ellen, daughter, unmarried, and Simon, died 1842, unmarried.

M – *cont.*   Mette, Jacques, 1801? – 1812.
Mette, Lisette, present at R. Forsyth's birth; witness.
Montplasier, Francis, 1806.

P   Pencenneau, Louis, 1812; petitioned Congress 1813; re-appeared
      1815 – 1817.
Pencenneau, Louis, Junr., son of Louis.
Pilette, Angelica, 1788? – 1806; wife of Louis and only child of
      Francis Wilette; married (2) Laframboise; probably married
      (3) Bartholomew Fortier; lived St. Clair Co. 1849.
Pilette, Hypolite, born 1799 of Louis.
Pilette, Louis, –1799 – 1812.

R   Raboin, Baptiste, 1803 – 1809.
Raboin (?) Margaret, wife of J. B. Gervais, heir and probably
      daughter of Raboin.
Racine, Francis, 1801 – 1812; petitioned Congress 1813.
Racine, Francis Junr., 1801 – 1812; born 1794; petitioned
      Congress 1813; married Madame Defond, widow of John B.
Roi, Antoine, 1793 – 1798; brother of Simon.
Roi, Catherine, daughter of Simon; married to Baltzare Latour;
      removed to St. Clair Co.
Roi, Marie, daughter of Simon; married to Touissant Gondrion;
      removed to St. Clair Co.
Roi, Simon, 1794 – 1803; married 1799 Madame Le Doux, widow
      of Charles.
Roque, Augustine, 1779 – 1789+; granted 400 acres "near Pioria."
Roque, Augustine, Junr.

S   Saint Dennis, Antoine, – 1812; witness 1820.
Soulard, Tousant, 1778; witness 1820.

T   Truteau, Jyte; signed letter to Rocheblave Jan. 28, 1778.

U   Urquette, _____ (Parquette ?) 1778 – 1793.

V   Val. Amable; signed letter to Rocheblave Jan. 26, 1778.
Venault, Joseph; signed letter to Rocheblave Jan. 26, 1778.
Verinat, Joseph; signed letter to Rocheblave Jan. 26, 1778.

W   Whitby, _____, 1801.
Wilette, Francis, 1788 or 1789; died 1804.
Wilette, Madame, wife of Francis; died about 1806.
Wilette, Angelica, daughter of Francis (see Pilette).

Note 5:   Thirteen dwellers of New Peoria on Dec. 20, 1813, petioned
Congress for relief on account of losses suffered in burning of
village and eviction of 42 inhabitants by Capt. Thomas E. Craig
of the Ill. Ter. militia in November, 1812. Congress under act

approved May 15, 1820, directed the register of the land office at Edwardsville, Ill., to examine and report on Claims at Peoria. Edward Cole, the register, afterward governor, heard witnesses and reported on 70 claims filed by 31 claimants. Congress under act approved March 3, 1823, confirmed claims with minor limitations. Surveys were not approved until 1840. American settlers had occupied lands. Suits for possession followed. Thirteen cases went to U. S. Supreme Court. Cash settlements ended the last litigation over these "French Claims" in 1867.

Note 6:   Ten dwellers "at the Pees" signed a joint letter to Rocheblave, last British governor at Fort Gage, Jan. 26, 1778, assuring him of their "most humble respect and submission." They acknowledged Rocheblave's previous letter to F. Maillet, evidently directing him to obtain sumission of "Mascoutin Chiefs."

Trading House — After 1812

Also called Opa post and the old French Trading post. (Situated on the east bank of the Illinois river in Tazewell County 3 miles southwardly from present Franklin street bridge, Peoria)

A   Alscomb, Antoine, 1825; tax assess. $50; father of Josette.
Alscomb, Josette, daughter of Antoine; married May 19, 1826, to Francis Bourbonne, Junr.; divorced him on charge of desertion June 2, 1829.

B   Bebeau, Louis, 1818; American Fur Co. employee.
Beabor, Louis, 1825; tax assess. $700.
Bourbonne, Antoine, voted 1825; independent trader; agent American Fur Co.; same at Kankakee river; lived Portage des Sioux, Mo. 1838.
Bourbonne, Catishe, wife of Francis, Sr.
Bourbonne, Francis, 1825, 1826; tax assess. $200; licensed 1825 to keep tavern with son, Francis.
Bourbonne, Francis, Junr., licensed to keep tavern as above; tax assess. $100; married May 19, 1826, Josette Alscomb.
Buisson, Louis, 1818 – 1828+; American Fur Co. agent.
Buisson, Madame, Pottawatomie Indian, wife of Louis.
Buisson, Mary, daughter of Louis; married to Anderson; removed to Leavenworth, Kan., 1845.

C   Chevelire (Chavelier?) Pierre, 1825.

D   Dullioriee, Andevine; voted 1825.
Deschamps, Antoine, 1818 – 1826+; Illinois manager, American Fur Co.

L   La Booncan, Eubelle; voted 1825.
        Landri, Pierre, slain 1825 by No-ma-que, an Indian.

M   Marsecau, Touissant; voted 1825.
        Mette, Jacques; court interpreter, 1825.
        Mette, Marie Louise, nee Dervin, wife of Jacques.

O   Ogee, Joseph, French Indian; came from Fort Clark where he was in 1821; rented cabin to Peoria Co. for court house, 1825; removed about 1828 to Rock River (now Dixon, Ill.); left there soon.
        Ogee, Madeline, Pottawatomie Indian, wife of Joseph; they separated; she married (2) Joe Alcott; removed to Kansas with Pottawatomies.
        Ogee, John, son of Joseph.

T   Tromley, _____, trader; removed to Kansas 1844.

• • •

(Peter Dumont, assessed $50 in 1825, lived at Little Detroit, the narrows).

Bibliography   American State Papers, Public Lands, Vols. I, II, III.
Annals, Ninth Congress, U. S.
U. S. Statutes at large 3, pp. 605, 786.
U. S. Supreme court reports, (15 Howard 357).
Public records of Peoria County.
Illinois Historical Society Publications, Nos. 6, 9, 37.
Illinois Historical Society Collections, Volume XXI.
Pioneers of Illinois (Matson).
History of Peoria (Drown, 1851).
Early Days of Peoria and Chicago (McCulloch).
Davenport Past and Present (Wilkie).
Life of Gurdon S. Hubbard (Hamilton).
Historical Encyclopedia of Illinois (Bateman and Selby).
History of Tazewell County (Chapman).
My Own Times, and Pioneer History of Illinois (Reynolds).
Indiana Historic Society Publications, No. 3, Volume III.
Wau-Bun (Kinzie).

Indians watch the two birch bark canoes of the Jolliet and Marquette
expedition as they enter the Mississippi River from the Wisconsin. 1673;
Diorama; The University of Iowa Museum of Natural History, Iowa City.

PLATE I

Arrival of Jolliet and Marquette at the Village of the Kaskaskia at Starved Rock. 1673; Robert A. Thom; Illinois State Historical Library, Springfield, Illinois; Painted in 1967.

ROBERT THOM

PLATE II

Launching of the Griffon on Lake Erie. 1679;
George Catlin; National Gallery of Art, Washington;
Paul Mellon Collection "1965"; Painted in 1847-1848.

PLATE III

La Salle and Party Arrive at the Village of the Illinois at Lake Peoria. January 4, 1680; George Catlin; National Gallery of Art, Washington; Paul Mellon Collection "1965"; Painted in 1847-1848.

PLATE IV

*La Salle's Party Feasted in the Illinois Village at Lake Peoria. January, 1680;
George Catlin; National Gallery of Art, Washington; Paul Mellon Collection "1965";
Painted in 1847-1848.*

PLATE V

• *La Salle Returns to Fort Frontenac by Sled. March, 1680;*
George Catlin; National Gallery of Art, Washington; Paul Mellon Collection "1965";
Painted in 1847-1848.

PLATE VI

Henri de Tonti Sues for Peace with the Iroquois at the Village of the Kaskaskia at Starved Rock. September, 1680; George Catlin; National Gallery of Art, Washington; Paul Mellon Collection "1965"; Painted in 1847-1848.

PLATE VII

La Salle Descends the Illinois on the Ice. January, 1682;
George Catlin; National Gallery of Art, Washington; Paul Mellon Collection "1965";
Painted in 1847-1848.

PLATE VIII

La Salle's Party Enters the Mississippi in Canoes. February 6, 1682;
George Catlin; National Gallery of Art, Washington; Paul Mellon Collection "1965";
Painted in 1847-1848.

PLATE IX

La Salle Claims Louisiana for France. April 9, 1682;
George Catlin; National Gallery of Art, Washington; Paul Mellon Collection "1965";
Painted in 1847-1848.

PLATE X

• *Illinois Indians in New Orleans in 1735. The seated woman at the left is a Fox Indian.*
Desseins de sauvages de plusieurs nations, Nouvelle Orleans, 1735.
Colored pen-and-ink sketch by Alexandre de Batz;
Peabody Museum, Harvard University; Photograph by Hillel Burger.

PLATE XI

No English, a Dandy. Peoria, 1830;
George Catlin; National Museum of American Art;
Smithsonain Institution; Gift of Mrs. Joseph Harrison, Jr.

Man Who Tracks, a Chief; Peoria. 1830;
George Catlin; National Museum of American Art; Smithsonian Institution;
Gift of Mrs. Joseph Harrison, Jr.

● *Henri de Tonti, founder of Peoria, at Pimœtoui, 1691-93.*
Lonnie Eugene Stewart, 1990;
Peoria 1691 Foundation.

PLATE XIII

Parrot of Carolina. Mark Catesby (1731-43); The Royal Collection©; Her Majesty Queen Elizabeth II; Windsor Castle.

PLATE XIV

•
This reconstruction of Fort Crèvecoeur, built near the original site of the fort in 1980, and operated by Fort Crèvecoeur, Inc., is open to the public.

•
Of the many places that have been suggested over the years as the original site of Fort Crèvecoeur, the one suggested by Arthur Lagron in 1913 best fits the most reliable evidence. The site is today in the P. and P. U. Railway Yards, at the point in the photograph where the road crosses the tracks.

• Aerial view of Peoria today. The reconstruction of Fort Crèvecoeur is in the foreground. (The proposed actual site is under the railroad tracks near the slough.) Old Peoria Village was in the area at the top right of the photograph. New Peoria Village was where the downtown area is today. The Trading House settlement was in the area just off the photograph at the lower left. Skyflick, Peoria.

PLATE XVI

Selected Bibliography

This bibliography is not a record of all sources consulted in the research for this book, but is meant as a guide to those interested in further pursuing the topics touched upon here. Many original documents are in the "Archives du Ministère des Affaires Étrangères" and other repositories in Paris. The Library of Congress has microfilm records of much of this material.

We have included a variety of basic works that will lead one to other good sources. We have included some, such as Margry's five volume collection of documents and Hennepin's "Description of Louisiana," which are dependable at least in part. We have excluded others such as Tonti's supposed second memoir which is wholly spurious.

Original Accounts and Compilations

Anderson, Melville B.
1898   *Relation of Henri de Tonty Concerning the Explorations of LaSalle from 1678 to 1683*. The Caxton Club, Chicago.

Bossu, Jean-Bertrand
1962   *Travels in the Interior of North America*. Edited by Seymor Feiler. University of Oklahoma Press, Norman.

Cadillac, Lamothe and Pierre de Liette
1947   *The Western Country in the 17th Century*. Edited by Milo Quaife. The Lakeside Press, Chicago.

Charlevoix, Pierre de
1966   *Journal of a Voyage to North America*. Readex Microprint Corp.

Collot, Victor
1909   *A Journey in North America*. Transactions of the Illinois State Historical Society, No. 13, pp. 269 – 298. Illinois State Historical Society, Springfield.

PAGE
107

French, B. F. (Ed.)
1846   *Historical Collections of Louisiana, Embracing many Rare and Valuable Documents Relating to the Natural, Civil and Political History of that State*. Wiley and Putnam, New York.

Hennepin, Louis
1966   *A Description of Louisiana*. Edited by John Gilmary Shea. Readex Microprint Corp.

Hutchins, Thomas
1904   *A Topographical Description of Virginia, Pennsylvania, Maryland, and North Carolina*. Edited by Frederick Charles Hicks. The Burrows Brothers Company, Cleveland.

Joutel, Henri
1966   *A Journal of the Last Voyage Performed by Monsieur de la Sale*. Readex Microprint Corp.

Kellogg, Louise Phelps (Ed.)
1953   *Early Narratives of the Northwest 1634 – 1699*. Barnes & Noble, Inc., New York.

Kenton, Edna (Ed.)
1927   *The Indians of North America*. Vol. 2. Harcourt, Brace & Company, New York.

Margry, Pierre (Ed.)
1876 – 1888   *Découvertes et Établissements des français dans l'Ouest et dans le Sud de l'Amerique Septentrionale, 1614 – 1754: Mémoires et Documents originaux*. Paris.

Pease, Theodore Calvin and Raymond C. Werner (Eds.)
1934   *The French Foundations 1680 – 1693*. Illinois Historical Collections, Vol. 23. Illinois State Historical Library, Springfield.

Shea, John Gilmary (Ed.)
1861   *Early Voyages Up and Down the Mississippi*. Joel Munsell, Albany.

1853   *Discovery and Exploration of the Mississippi Valley*. Redfield, New York.

Temple, Wayne C. (Ed.)
1975   *Indian Villages of the Illinois Country*. Illinois State Museum Scientific Papers, Supplement to Vol. 2, Part 1, Atlas. Illinois State Museum, Springfield.

Thwaites, Reuben Gold (Ed.)
1902 – 1908   *Collections of the State Historical Society of Wisconsin*. Vol. 16 to 18. Democrat Printing Company, Madison.

1896 – 1901   *The Jesuit Relations and Allied Documents: Travel and Explorations of the Jesuit Missionaries in New France*. The Burrows Brothers Company, Cleveland.

Tucker, Sara Jones (Ed.)
1942   *Indian Villages of the Illinois Country*. Illinois State Museum Scientific Papers, Vol. 2, Pt. 1, Atlas. Illinois State Museum, Springfield.

Historic Indians of the Illinois Country

Edmunds, David R.
1978   *The Potawatomis: Keepers of the Fire*. University of Oklahoma Press, Norman.

Jablow, Joseph
1974   *Indians of Illinois and Indiana: Illinois, Kickapoo, and Potawatomi Indians*. Garland Publishing, Inc., New York and London.

Scott, James
1973   *The Illinois Nation*. Part 1. The Streator Historical Society, Streator, Illinois.

1976   *The Illinois Nation*. Part 2. The Streator Historical Society, Streator, Illinois.

1981   *The Potawatomi: Conquerors of Illinois*. The Streator Historical Society, Streator, Illinois.

Tanner, Helen Hornbeck
1987   *Atlas of Great Lakes Indian History*. University of Oklahoma Press, Norman.

Temple, Wayne C.
1966   *Indian Villages of the Illinois Country*. Illinois State Museum Scientific Papers, Vol. 2, Part II. Illinois State Museum, Springfield.

Trigger, Bruce G. (Ed.)
1978   *Handbook of North American Indians: The Northeast*. Vol. 15. Smithsonian Institution Press, Washington.

Valley, Doris and Mary M. Lembcke (Eds.)
1991   *The Peorias: A History of the Peoria Indian Tribe of Oklahoma*. The Peoria Indian Tribe of Oklahoma, Miami.

Vogelin, Erminie Wheeler and J. A. Jones
1974   *Indians of Western Illinois and Southern Wisconsin.* Garland
                Publishing, Inc., New York and London.

Walthall, John A. and Thomas E. Emerson (Eds.)
1992   *Calumet and Fleur-de-lys: Archaeology of Indian and French Contact
                in the Midcontinent.* Smithsonian Institution Press, Washington.

Overviews of the Period

Alvord, Clarence Walworth
1920   *The Illinois Country.* Centennial History of Illinois, Vol. 1. Illinois
                Centennial Commission, Springfield.

Alvord, Clarence Walworth and Clarence Carter (Eds.)
1917   *The Critical Period, 1672 – 1769.* Illinois Historical Collections,
                Vol. 10. Illinois State Historical Society, Springfield.

                The New Regime, 1675 – 1767. Illinois Historical Collections,
                Vol. 11. Illinois State Historical Society, Springfield.

Balance, Charles
1870   *The History of Peoria, Illinois.* N. C. Nason, Peoria.

Giraud, Marcel
1953 – 1987   *Histoire de la Lousiane Française. Presses Universitaires de France,
                Paris.* (The five volumes of this work cover the period from 1698
                – 1731. Volumes 1, 2, and 5 are available in English translation
                from Louisiana State University Press, Baton Rouge.)

Klein, Jerry
1985   *Peoria!* Visual Communications, Inc., Peoria.

Matson, Nehemiah
1882   *Pioneers of Illinois.* Knight and Leonard, Chicago.

Palm, Mary Borgias
1931   *The Jesuit Missions of the Illinois Country 1673 – 1763.* Ph.D
                dissertation, St. Louis University. The Sisters of Notre Dame,
                Cleveland.

Sauer, Carl O.
1980   *Seventeenth Century North America.* Netzahualcoyotl Historical
                Society, Berkeley.

Biographies

Adams, Arthur
1961   *The Explorations of Pierre Esprit Radisson*. Ross & Haines, Inc.,
            Minneapolis.

Brown, George W. (Ed.)
1967   *Dictionary of Canadian Biography*. Vol. 1 (1000 – 1700).
            University of Toronto Press, Toronto.

Brown, George W., David M. Hayne and Francess G. Halpenny (Eds.)
1974   *Dictionary of Canadian Biography*. Vol. 3 (1701 – 1740).
            University of Toronto Press, Toronto.

Ekberg, Carl J.
1991   *Marie Rouensa-8cate8a and the Foundations of French
            Illinois*. Illinois Historical Journal Vol. 84, No. 3, pp. 146 – 160.
            Illinois State Historical Society. Springfield.

Hayne, David M. (Ed.)
1969   *Dictionary of Canadian Biography*. Vol. 2 (1741 – 1770).
            University of Toronto Press, Toronto.

Murphy, Edmund Robert
1941   *Henry De Tonty: Fur Trader of the Mississippi*. Johns Hopkins
            Press, Baltimore.

Nute, Grace Lee
1978   *Caesars of the Wilderness*. Minnesota Historical Society Press, St.
            Paul.

Historical Accounts, Analyses, and Essays

Balesi, Charles J.
1992   *The Time of the French in the Heart of North America: 1673 –
            1818*. Alliance Française, Chicago.

Buisseret, David
1991   *Mapping the French Empire in North America*. Catalog of
            Exhibition. The Newberry Library, Chicago.

Delanglez, Jean
1938   *Some LaSalle Journeys*. Institute of Jesuit History, Chicago.

1939   *Frontenac and the Jesuits*. Institute of Jesuit History, Chicago.

1948   *Life and Voyages of Louis Jolliet, 1645 – 1700.* Institute of Jesuit History, Chicago.

Faye, Stanley (Ed.)
1945   *A Search for Copper on the Illinois River: The Journal of Legardeur Delisle.* Journal of the Illinois State Historical Society, Vol. 38, No. 1, pp. 38 – 57. Illinois State Historical Society, Springfield.

Fridley, Russel W. and Jean A. Brookings
1982   *Where Two Worlds Meet: The Great Lakes Fur Trade.* Catalogue of Exhibit. Minnesota Historical Society, St. Paul.

Galloway, Patricia K.
1982   *LaSalle and His Legacy: Frenchmen and Indians in the Lower Mississippi Valley.* University Press of Mississippi, Jackson.

Lagron, Arthur
1918   *Fort Crèvecoeur.* Journal of the Illinois State Historical Society, Vol. 5, No. 4, pp. 451 – 457. Illinois State Historical Society, Springfield.

McDermott, John Francis (Ed.)
1969   *Frenchmen and French Ways in the Mississippi Valley.* University of Illinois Press, Urbana.

Mulkey, Floyd
1944   *Fort St. Louis at Peoria.* Journal of Illinois State Historical Society, Vol. 37, pp. 301 – 316. Illinois State Historical Society, Springfield.

Nasatir, A. P.
1928   *The Anglo-Spanish Frontier in the Illinois Country During the American Revolution, 1779 – 1783.* Journal of the Illinois State Historical Society, Vol. 21, No. 3, pp. 291 – 358. Illinois State Historical Society, Springfield.

Parkman, Francis
1963   *The Discovery of the Great West: LaSalle.* Holt, Rinehart & Winston, New York.

Pease, Theodore Calvin and Ernestine Jenison (Eds.)
1940   *Illinois on the Eve of the Seven Years' War: 1747 – 1755.* Illinois Historical Collections, Vol. 29. Illinois State Historical Society, Springfield.

Wedel, Mildred Mott (Ed.)
1985   *A John Delanglez, S. J., Anthology.* Selections Useful for Mississippi Valley and Trans-Mississippi American Indian Studies. Garland Publishing, Inc., New York & London.

White, Richard

1991   *The Middle Ground: Indians, Empires, and Republics in the Great Lakes Region, 1659 – 1815.* Cambridge University Press, New York.

Sources on the French District

Alvord, Clarence Walworth

1909   *Kaskaskia Records: 1778 – 1790.* Illinois Historical Collections, Vol. 5. Illinois State Historical Library, Springfield.

1907   *Cahokia Records: 1778 – 1790.* Illinois Historical Collections, Vol. 2. Illinois State Historical Library, Springfield.

Belting, Natalia Maree

1975   *Kaskaskia Under the French Regime.* Polyanthos, New Orleans.

Brown, Margeret K. and Lawrie C. Dean (Eds.)

1977   *The Village of Chartres in Colonial Illinois: 1720 – 1765.* Polyanthos, New Orleans.

East, Ernest E.

1949   *Lincoln and the Peoria French Claims.* Journal of the Illinois State Historical Society. Vol. 42. pp. 41 – 56. Springfield.

Ekberg, Carl J.

1985   *Colonial Ste. Genevieve: An Adventure on the Mississippi Frontier.* Gerald, Missouri.

Ekberg, Carl J. and William E. Foley (Eds.)

1989   *An Account of Upper Lousiana by Nicolas de Finiels.* University of Missouri Press, Columbia.

Peterson, Charles E.

1993   *Colonial St. Louis: Building a Creole Capital.* The Patrice Press, Tucson.

Price, Anna

1982   *The French Regime in Illinois, 1718 – 1740.* Historic Illinois, Vol. 5. No. 3, pp. 1 – 5. Illinois Department of Conservation Division of Historic Sites, Springfield.

Snyder, John Francis

1962   *John Francis Snyder: Selected Writings.* Illinois State Historical Society, Springfield.

Illinois Country and Related French Period Archaeology

Barr, Keith L., et al.
1988   *Intensive Archaeological Explorations for Peoria's 18th Century French Village*. Illinois State University, Midwest Archaeological Research Center Report No. 7. Illinois State University, Normal.

Brain, Jeffrey P.
1979   *Tunica Treasure*. Harvard University, Salem.

Brown, James A.
1961   *The Zimmerman Site: A Report on Excavations at the Grand Village of Kaskaskia*. Illinois State Museum Report of Investigations, No. 9. Illinois State Museum, Springfield.

Brown, Margret Kimball
1975   *The Zimmerman Site: Further Excavations at the Grand Village of Kaskaskia*. Illinois State Museum Report of Investigations, No. 32. Illinois State Museum, Springfield.

Good, Mary Elizabeth
1972   *Guebert Site: An 18th Century Historic Kaskaskia Indian Village*. Central States Archaeological Society Memoir No. 2. Central States Archaeological Society, St. Louis.

Gums, Bonnie L.
1988   *Archaeology at French Colonial Cahokia*. Illinois Historic Preservation Agency Studies in Illinois Archaeology, No. 3, Springfield.

Hall, Robert L.
1991   *The Archaeology of La Salle's Fort St. Louis on Starved Rock and the Problems of the Newell Fort*. In French Colonial Archaeology, Edited by John A. Walthall. University of Illinois Press, Urbana.

Jelks, Edward B., Carl J. Ekberg and Terrance J. Martin
1989   *Excavations at the Laurens Site: Probable Location of Fort de Chartres I*. Illinois Historic Preservation Agency Studies in Illinois Archaeology, No. 5. Springfield.

Jelks, Edward B. and Joan Unsicker
1981   *Archaeological Assessment of Seven Sites Purported to be the Location of La Salle's Ft. Crèvecoeur*. Report prepared for the Illinois Department of Conservation, Springfield.

Quimby, George Irving
1966   *Indian Culture and European Trade Goods*. University of
                Wisconsin, Madison.

Walthall, John A. and Elizabeth D. Benchley
1987   *The River L'Abbe Mission*. Illinois Historic Preservation Agency
                Studies in Illinois Archaeology, No. 2. Springfield.

Walthall, John A.
1991   *French Colonial Archaeology: The Illinois Country and the Western
                Great Lakes*. University of Illinois Press, Urbana.

Westover, Allen Ray
1984   *A History of the Archaeological Investigations at Starved Rock,
                Illinois*. Unpublished masters thesis, Illinois State University,
                Normal.

Index

Note: Text references are in regular type; references to illustrations are in boldface.